PENGUIN BOOKS

ZERO DEGREES OF EMPATHY

'Fascinating information about the relation between
degrees of empathy and the state of our brains'
Terry Eagleton, *Financial Times*

'Rigorously researched . . . [Baron-Cohen's] discussion of how
parents can instill lifelong empathy in their children is particularly useful'
Psychology Today

'Baron-Cohen has made a major contribution to our
understanding of autism' Dorothy Rowe, *Guardian*

'Bold'
Ian Critchley, *Sunday Times*

'Engaging and informative'
Times Higher Education Supplement

'Fascinating and disturbing'
Alasdair Palmer, *Sunday Telegraph*

'Short, clear, and highly readable. Baron-Cohen guides you
through his complex material as if you were a student attending a
course of lectures. He's an excellent teacher; there's no excuse for not
understanding anything he says' *The Spectator*

'Fascinating and persuasive'
Daily Post

'Baron-Cohen is convincing that empathy and especially the lack of
empathy is a proper scientific subject and that neuroscience and
psychology can work together to help us understand some of the
material aspects of fellow feeling' *New Humanist*

'Simon Baron-Cohen combines his creative talent with
evidence and reason to make the case that evil is essentially a
failure of empathy. It is an understanding that can enlighten
an old debate and hold out the promise of new remedies'
Matt Ridley, author of *The Rational Optimist*

'Isn't it lucky . . . that the very people who can't put themselves into
other people's shoes, have a champion [in Simon Baron-Cohen]
who, by dint of his curiosity, has turned it into an art form?'
Lee Randall, *The Scotsman*

'The author conveys brain research with verve'
Science Focus

ABOUT THE AUTHOR

Simon Baron-Cohen is Professor at Cambridge University in the fields of psychology and psychiatry. He is also the Director of the Autism Research Centre there. He has carried out research into social neuroscience over a thirty-year career. His popular science book *The Essential Difference* (Penguin 2003) has been translated in over a dozen languages, and has been widely reviewed.

SIMON BARON-COHEN

Zero Degrees of Empathy

A new theory of human cruelty and kindness

PENGUIN BOOKS

PENGUIN BOOKS

Published by the Penguin Group
Penguin Books Ltd, 80 Strand, London WC2R ORL, England
Penguin Group (USA), Inc., 375 Hudson Street, New York, New York 10014, USA
Penguin Group (Canada), 90 Eglinton Avenue East, Suite 700, Toronto, Ontario, Canada M4P 2Y3
(a division of Pearson Penguin Canada Inc.)
Penguin Ireland, 25 St Stephen's Green, Dublin 2, Ireland (a division of Penguin Books Ltd)
Penguin Group (Australia), 707 Collins Street, Melbourne, Victoria 3008, Australia
(a division of Pearson Australia Group Pty Ltd)
Penguin Books India Pvt Ltd, 11 Community Centre, Panchsheel Park, New Delhi – 110 017, India
Penguin Group (NZ), 67 Apollo Drive, Rosedale, Auckland 0632, New Zealand
(a division of Pearson New Zealand Ltd)
Penguin Books (South Africa) (Pty) Ltd, Block D, Rosebank Office Park,
181 Jan Smuts Avenue, Parktown North, Gauteng 2193, South Africa

Penguin Books Ltd, Registered Offices: 80 Strand, London WC2R ORL, England

www.penguin.com

First published by Allen Lane 2011
Published in Penguin Books 2012

010

Copyright © Simon Baron-Cohen, 2011

The moral right of the author has been asserted

Grateful acknowledgement is given to the following to reproduce photographs:
882 IAM/akg/World History Archive (inmates in Dachau (p. 2)); Harvard Widener Library &
Central Zionist Archives (Martin Buber (p. 5)); Jeff J. Mitchell/Getty Images
(Capuchin monkeys (p. 100)); Benny Gool (Desmond Tutu (p. 128))

Typeset by Jouve (UK), Milton Keynes
Printed in Great Britain by Clays Ltd, St Ives plc

A CIP catalogue record for this book is available from the British Library

ISBN: 978-0-141-01796-9

www.greenpenguin.co.uk

MIX
Paper from
responsible sources
FSC
www.fsc.org
FSC® C018179

Penguin Books is committed to a sustainable
future for our business, our readers and our planet.
This book is made from Forest Stewardship
Council™ certified paper.

In memory of

Peter Lipton (1950–2007)
Professor of Philosophy of Science, Cambridge University,
who combined precision in explanation with
humour and compassion

and

Judy Ruth Baron Cohen (née Greenblatt) (1933–2008)
who gave her five children and five grandchildren
their internal pot of gold

Contents

Acknowledgements

This book isn't for people with a sensitive disposition. You can't write about human cruelty in a cheerful way, so if you're looking for a fun read proceed no further. In this book I attempt to redefine 'evil' in terms of the erosion of *empathy*, and look at why some people have more or less empathy than others, and what happens when we lose it. Empathy is not the only component that contributes to cruelty but I argue it is the final common pathway. I argue that empathy erosion is necessary but not sufficient for cruelty to take place. Distressing and even shocking as the material may be, the nature of empathy is (to me, at least) endlessly fascinating, and the research behind it has been exciting (an odd choice of word in the circumstances), primarily because I have such a wonderful group of talented scientists as colleagues. I am pleased to have the chance to thank them here.

Scientists collect bizarre things (Darwin famously collected beetles and finches). In our case, as empathy researchers, we collected emotions! Our DVD *Mindreading*[1] is where we house all 412 of them. Ofer Golan, Sally Wheelwright, Jacqueline Hill and I developed this electronic library, and Ofer Golan, Emma Ashwin, Yael Granader, Kimberly Armstrong, Gina Owens, Nic Lever, Jon Drori, Nick Paske, Claire Harcup and I also developed a second DVD (*The Transporters*[2]) as a fun way to teach empathy to preschool children with autism who struggle to achieve this.

Scientists also develop new ways to measure things. For us, the challenge was to come up with new ways to measure individual differences in empathy. First, Sally Wheelwright, Carrie Allison, Bonnie Auyeung and I developed the Empathy Quotient (EQ). You'll find this in Appendix 1. To track down where empathy might be hiding in the brain, Chris Ashwin, Bhismadev Chakrabarti, Mike Lombardo, John Suckling, Ed Bullmore, Meng-Chuan Lai, Matthew Belmonte,

Jac Billington, John Herrington, Howard Ring, Steve Williams, Marie Gomot, Ilaria Minio-Paluello and I conducted brain-scanning studies. To investigate 'the trouble with testosterone'[3] and its impact on empathy, Bonnie Auyeung, Rebecca Knickmeyer, Emma Ashwin (née Chapman), Svetlana Lutchmaya, Liliana Ruta, Erin Ingudomnukul, Lindsay Chura, Kevin Taylor, Peter Raggat, Gerald Hackett and I collected amniotic fluid from babies and blood samples from adults. Bhismadev Chakrabarti, Frank Dudbridge, Sharmila Basu, Carrie Allison, Sally Wheelwright, Grant Hill-Cawthorne, Lindsey Kent and I also hunted for 'empathy genes'. All of these projects have been fascinating.

Keeping a busy research lab running smoothly while writing a book assumes wonderful administrative support: Gaenor Moore, Paula Naimi, Jenny Hannah, Carol Farmer and Rachel Jackson have been an amazing admin team. Gaenor also cheerfully compiled the references for this book, no small feat, for which I am extremely grateful. Bhismadev Chakrabarti and Mike Lombardo both generously commented on draft chapters in this book. Mike in particular taught me more social neuroscience and Bhisma taught me more genetics during this process, which was invaluable.

Helen Conford and Stefan McGrath at Penguin UK have been patiently waiting for this book since 2004! Helen gave me insightful, careful feedback as the book took shape. It took six years to write because the hunt for 'empathy genes' is not quick. Katinka Matson and John Brockman, my agents, showed the same remarkable patience in waiting for this book to be born. I am indebted to Charlotte Ridings and Jan Kristiannson for their excellent editorial suggestions, and to Thomas Keheller at Basic Books for his support.

I give special thanks to Bridget Lindley for all her support, to my parents (Judy and Vivian) and siblings (Dan, Ash, Liz and Suzie) for their dependable humour, and to my children, Sam, Kate and Robin, for their playfulness and encouragement. I hope I gave them enough of the 'internal pot of gold' that I got from my parents, who got it from theirs.

Preface

I have been studying empathy for thirty years, and my aim now is to put this remarkable substance on to the table so we can all look at it from every angle. In my first book, *Mindblindness*, I focused on one part of the nature of empathy (the part related to how we understand other people, that is, the 'cognitive' part of empathy) and on the case of autism, where difficulties with cognitive empathy abound. In my second book, *The Essential Difference*, I included the second part of empathy (the part related to our emotional reactions to people, that is, the 'affective' part of empathy), and on how the two sexes differ in empathy. In that book I again explored the flip side of empathy, with an analysis of the difficulties people with autism face in acquiring this essential skill.

Now, in *Zero Degrees of Empathy*, I examine how some people become capable of cruelty, and whether a loss of affective empathy inevitably has this consequence. This book goes deeper into the subject than I have gone before, by drilling down into the brain basis of empathy and looking at its social and biological determinants, and it is broader too, by having a close look at some of the medical conditions that lead to a loss of empathy. My main goal is to understand human cruelty, replacing the unscientific term 'evil' with the term 'empathy' erosion. Unlike some of my earlier books, this one is not about autism (though in passing we look at why people with autism tend not to be cruel despite their empathy difficulties). And in looking at some of the medical conditions that involve a loss of empathy, the point is not that these conditions are the main causes of cruelty (far from it), but they afford us an opportunity to look at the special circuits in the brain that ordinarily enable empathy. To be clear, cruelty is sadly all too common in society, not just a feature of some rare medical conditions. In this book, we get a glimpse of the many factors, both social and biological, that can impact our empathy.

Those readers who wish to pursue the subject in more depth will find the relevant scientific papers (indicated by Arabic numbers) listed in the References starting on page 156. Points that are explained further in the Notes section are indicated by Roman numerals and can be found on pages 148–155.

I

Explaining 'Evil' and Human Cruelty

When I was seven years old, my father told me the Nazis had turned Jews into lampshades. Just one of those comments that you hear once and the thought never goes away. To a child's mind – even to an adult's – these two types of thing just don't belong together. He also told me the Nazis turned Jews into bars of soap.

This rumour was based in part on testimonies from an eyewitness account from a survivor at Buchenwald concentration camp. Billy Wilder's 1945 documentary included footage of such a lampshade, a possession of Ilse Koch, wife of the commandant, and known as the Witch of Buchenwald. Such rumours were fuelled by the piece of tattooed human skin with pin holes around the perimeter held at the National Museum of Health and Medicine in Washington DC.

Whatever the truth of this story, I knew our family was Jewish, so this image of turning people into objects felt a bit close to home.

My father also told me about one of his former girlfriends, Ruth Goldblatt,[i] whose mother had survived a concentration camp. He had been introduced to the mother and was shocked to discover that her hands were reversed. Nazi scientists had severed Mrs Goldblatt's hands, switched them around and sewn them on again so that, if she put her hands out palms down, her thumbs were on the outside and her little fingers were on the inside. Just one of the many 'experiments' they had conducted. I realized there was a paradox at the heart of human nature – that people could objectify others – which my young mind was not yet ready to figure out.

Years later, I was teaching at St Mary's Hospital Medical School in London. I sat in on a lecture on physiology. The professor was teaching about human adaptation to temperature. He told the students the best data available on human adaptation to extreme cold had been collected by Nazi scientists performing 'immersion experiments' on Jews and other inmates of Dachau Concentration Camp, who they put into vats of freezing water. They collected systematic data on how heart rate correlated with time, at zero degrees centigrade.[4] Hearing about this unethical research[ii] retriggered that same question in my mind: *how can humans treat other people as objects?* How do humans come to switch off their natural feelings of sympathy for a fellow-human being who is suffering?

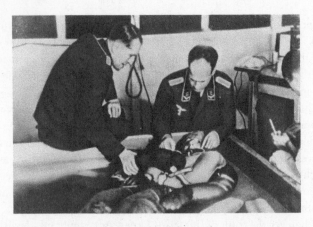

Figure 1: Inmates in Dachau Concentration Camp subjected to a 'cold water immersion experiment'. The experiment aimed to see if they could stay in freezing water for up to three hours. (On the left is Professor Ernst Holzlohner, and on the right is Dr Sigmund Rasher.)

These examples are particularly shocking because they involve educated doctors and scientists (professions we are brought up to trust) performing inhumane experiments or operations. We have to assume these doctors were not being cruel for the sake of it. I (generously) assume the scientists doing the immersion experiments wanted to contribute to medical knowledge, to know, for example, how to help victims rescued after being shipwrecked in icy seas. Even the Nazi doctors who had sewn poor Mrs Goldblatt's hands back to front were not (I assume) motivated to do cruel things for cruelty's sake: they too were presumably following their scientific impulse, wanting to understand how to test the limits of micro-surgical procedures.

What these scientists lost sight of, in their quest for knowledge, was the humanity of their 'subjects'. It is an irony that the human sciences describe their objects of study as 'subjects', since this implies sensitivity to the feelings of the person being studied. In practice, the feelings of the subjects in these experiments were of no concern. Nazi laws defined Jews as genetically sub-human and ordered their extermination, as part of the eugenics programme of the time. Within this political framework, 'using' the inmates of concentration camps as 'subjects' in medical research might even have seemed to these doctors to be ethical, if it contributed knowledge for the greater good.

Cruelty for its own sake *was* a part of ordinary Nazi guards' behaviour. Sadly, there is no shortage of horrific examples, and I have selected just one from the biography of Thomas Buergenthal.[5] At just nine years old, Thomas was rounded up with thousands of Jews and taken to Auschwitz. There he had to watch while an inmate was forced to hang his friend who had tried to escape. The SS guard ordered the inmate to put a noose around his friend's neck. The man couldn't fulfil the order because his hands were shaking so much, with fear and distress. His friend turned to him, took the noose and, in a remarkable act, kissed his friend's hand, and then put the noose around his own neck. Angrily, the SS guard kicked the chair away from under the man to be hanged.

Nine-year-old Thomas and the other inmates, watching the man kissing his friend's hand, rejoiced at that simple act that said (without words), 'I will not let my friend be forced to kill me.' Thomas survived Auschwitz (perhaps because his father taught him to stand close to the shed when Dr Mengele was making his selection of those who would die[iii]) and described this story in his book *A Lucky Child*.[6] The empathy within the friendship comes through so powerfully in this awful situation, as does the extreme lack of empathy of the guard. If the aim was to punish or to set an example, the guard could have just shot the escapee himself. Presumably he chose this particular form of punishment because he *wanted* the two friends to suffer.

Today, almost half a century after my father's revelations to me about the extremes of human behaviour, my mind is still exercised by the same, single objective: to understand human cruelty. What greater reason for writing a book than the persistence of a single question that can gnaw away in one's mind all of one's conscious life? What other question could take root in such an unshakeable way? I presume the reason why I find myself returning to this question again and again is because the question of how human beings can ignore the humanity of others *begs* an answer – yet answers are not forthcoming. Or at least, those answers that are supplied are in some way unsatisfying. If the answers were sufficient, the question would feel as if it had been answered and the matter settled. There would be no need to restlessly and repeatedly return to it. Clearly, better answers are still needed.

The standard explanation is that the Holocaust (sadly echoed, as we shall see, in many cultures historically across the globe) is an example of the 'evil' that humans are capable of inflicting on one another. Evil is treated as incomprehensible, a topic that cannot be dealt with because the scale of the horror is so great that nothing can convey its enormity. The standard view turns out to be widely held, and indeed the concept of evil is used as an explanation for such awful behaviour:

Why did the murderer kill an innocent child? Because he was evil.

Why did this terrorist become a suicide-bomber? Because she was evil.

But, when you hold up the concept of evil to examine it, it is no explanation at all. For a scientist this is, of course, wholly inadequate. What the Nazis (and others like them) did was unimaginably terrible. But that doesn't mean we should simply shut down enquiry into how people are capable of behaving in such ways, or use a non-explanation, saying such people are simply evil.

As a scientist I want to understand the factors causing people to treat others as if they are mere objects. In this book I explore how people can treat each other cruelly, *not* with reference to the concept of evil, but with reference to the concept of *empathy*. We shall see that empathy is not the only component, but I argue it is the final 'common pathway' to cruelty. Unlike the concept of evil, empathy has explanatory power. In the coming chapters I put empathy under the microscope.

TURNING PEOPLE INTO OBJECTS

The challenge is to explain how people are capable of causing extreme hurt to one another without resorting to the all-too-easy concept of evil. So let's substitute the term 'evil' with the term 'empathy erosion'. Empathy erosion can arise because of corrosive emotions, such as bitter resentment, or desire for revenge, or blind hatred, or desire to protect. In theory these are transient emotions, the empathy erosion reversible. Equally, empathy erosion can occur as a result of the beliefs we hold (such as the belief that a class of person is unworthy of human rights); or because of the goals we have (such as defending our country), or because of our intentions (for example to make an employee redundant). Empathy erosion can even occur as a result of fear (of the danger of standing up against a bully) or obedience to authority (so clearly demonstrated in Stanley Milgram's experiment at Yale where volunteers were willing to 'electrocute' someone under orders from a man in a white coat). Empathy erosion can just be the result of wanting to conform (as shown in Philip Zimbardo's Stanford Prison experiment where students assigned to be the prison guards soon started acting aggressively). Again, all of these lapses of empathy are in principle transient and reversible. But empathy erosion can also be the result of more permanent psychological characteristics.

The insight that underlying empathy erosion is *people turning people into objects* goes back at least to Martin Buber, an Austrian philosopher who resigned his professorship at the University of Frankfurt in 1933, when Hitler came to power. The title of his famous book is *Ich und Du* (*I and Thou*).[7] He contrasted the Ich-Du (I-You) mode of being (where you are connecting with another person, as a person with thoughts and feelings, acknowledging their subjectivity, as an end in itself) with the Ich-Es (I-It) mode of being (where you are treating the person as an object, ignoring their subjectivity, so as to use them for some purpose). He argued that the latter mode of treating a person was devaluing.

Figure 2: Martin Buber

When our empathy is switched off, we are solely in the 'I' mode. In such a state we relate only to things, or to people *as if they were just things*. Most of us are capable of doing this occasionally. We might be quite capable of focusing on our work without sparing a thought for the homeless person on the street outside our office. But, whether we are in this state transiently or permanently, there is no 'thou' visible – at least, not a 'thou' with different thoughts and feelings. Treating other people as if they were just objects is one of the worst things you can do to another human being, to ignore their subjectivity, their thoughts and feelings.

When a person is solely focused on the pursuit of their own interests they have all the potential to be unempathic. At best, in this state, they are in a world of their own and their behaviour will have little negative impact on others. They might end up in this state of mind because of years of resentment and hurt (often the result of conflict) or, as we shall see, for more enduring, neurological reasons. (Interestingly, in this state of single-minded pursuit of one's own goals, one's project might even have a positive focus: helping people, for example. But even if a person's project is positive, worthy and valuable, if it is singleminded, it is by definition unempathic.[iv])

So, now we've made a specific move: aiming to explain how people can be cruel to each other not out of evil but because of empathy erosion. While that feels marginally more satisfying as an answer (it is at least the beginning of an explanation), it is still far from a complete answer. That's because it begs the further questions of *what* empathy is, and *how* it can be eroded. But at least these are tractable questions, and ones we shall attempt to answer as we proceed through this book.

By the end of our journey, there should be less of a nagging need for answers to the big question of understanding human cruelty. The mind should be quieted if the answers are beginning to feel satisfying. But before we delve into the nature of empathy let's look at a handful of factual examples from around the world, to prove that the awful things the Nazis did were *not* unique to the Nazis. We have to go through this if only to eliminate one (in my opinion) absurd view, which is that the Nazis were in some way uniquely cruel. As you'll see, they weren't.

EMPATHY EROSION AROUND THE GLOBE

Erosion of empathy is a state of mind that can be found in any culture. In 2006 I was in Kenya with my family on holiday. We landed in Nairobi, a massive international city, swirling with people. Nairobi is sadly home to one of the largest slums in Africa. People sleeping on the streets, mothers dying of AIDS, malnourished children begging or doing anything they can to survive. I met Esther, a young Kenyan woman, one of the fortunate ones who had a job. She warned me to be careful of the rising crime in Nairobi.

'I was in the supermarket,' she said. 'Suddenly, a woman near me who was queuing to pay for her groceries let out a scream. A man behind her had *cut off* her finger. In the commotion, the man slid the wedding ring off the severed finger, and ran off into the crowds. It all happened so quickly.'

This is a shocking example of what one person can do to another. Some people question whether such an event could be true, given the difficulty of cutting through a bone, but let's for a moment assume it is true (and I had no reason to suspect Esther was lying). Medically, we know fingers can be cut off. Let's try to imagine what it takes to commit such an act. Formulating the plan to go out into the crowded supermarket to steal is easy enough to comprehend, especially if you are starving. Formulating the plan to take a knife with you is a bit harder to identify with, since it indicates clear premeditation to cut something.

But for me the key moment is to imagine the mind of the person in the seconds just before committing the act of cutting. At that very moment, presumably all that is visible to the thief is the target (the ring), a small object that could feed him for weeks. All that is lying between him and his next meal is the woman's finger that has to be severed. The fact that the finger is attached to a hand is mere inconvenience, and cold logic points to the solution: detach it. The fact that the hand is attached to a person, with her own life and her own feelings, is at that moment irrelevant. Out of mind. It is an example of *turning another person into (no more than) an object.* My argument is that when you treat someone as an object, your empathy has been turned off.

The above example might suggest that someone capable of this crime had a momentary blip. Could the perpetrator's desperation, hunger and poverty have been so overwhelming that he temporarily lost his empathy for the victim? We have all experienced, or observed in others, such transient states, where afterwards one's empathy recovers. I'm guessing that during your transient lapses in empathy nothing as awful happens as we saw in this example. This suggests that what this man did to this woman was *more* than a transient lapse. My concern in this book is with this more enduring phenomenon – the result of more stable traits where it is harder, if not impossible, to recover one's empathy, and where the consequences can be extremely serious. We will have a close look at people in the population who desperately need empathy, but who for various reasons don't have it – and probably never will.

More of that later. For now, I am going to limit myself to four other examples of empathy erosion around the planet, because you don't need lots of distressing examples to have proof that this can happen in any culture.

This next example concerns Josef Fritzl, who built a cellar in his home in Amstetten in northern Austria. You probably heard about this case, since it made worldwide headline news.[8] On 24 August 1984 he imprisoned his daughter Elisabeth down in the cellar and kept her there for twenty-four years, telling his wife she had gone missing. He raped Elisabeth – day after day – from the age of eleven and well into her young adulthood. She ended up having seven children in the basement prison, one of whom died aged three days old, and whose body her father (the child's father and grandfather) burned to dispose of the evidence. Imagine, burning your grandchild.

Repeatedly during those twenty-four years, Josef and his wife

Rosemarie appeared on Austrian television, apparently distressed by Elisabeth's disappearance, appealing to the public to help them trace her. Josef, now aged seventy-three, claimed that three of the children mysteriously turned up on his doorstep, abandoned by their mother, and he and his wife (their grandmother) raised them. The other three children grew up in the basement prison, ending up with major psychological disturbance. How could a father treat his daughter as an object and deprive her and three of his children/grandchildren of their right to freedom in this way? *Where was his empathy?*

The next example of empathy erosion which stopped me in my tracks was a report on the BBC[9] from Uganda. Rebel soldiers came into the village of Pajong. It was 24 July 2002. Esther Rechan was a young mother who described what happened:

> My two-year-old was sitting on the veranda. The rebels started kicking him. They kicked him to death ... I had my five-year-old with me, when the female rebel commander ordered all of us with children to pick them up and smash them against the veranda poles. We had to hit them until they were dead. All of us with children, we had to kill them. If you did it slowly they would beat you and force you to hit your children harder, against the poles. In all, seven children were killed by their mothers like that. My own child was only five.[v]

What was going through the minds of these rebel soldiers, that they could force a mother to batter her own child to death?

Now consider an example from a lesser-known holocaust, one *not* committed by the Nazis. I heard about this when I went to Turkey last summer. The Turks are renowned for their warm, welcoming, friendly culture but, when Turkey was under Ottoman rule, they regarded Christian ethnic Armenians as second-class citizens. As far back as the 1830s, for example, Armenians were not eligible to give testimony against Muslims in court – their evidence was considered 'inadmissible'. By the 1870s the Armenians were pressing for reforms, and during the 1890s at least 100,000 of them were killed. On 24 April 1915, 250 Armenian intellectuals were rounded up, imprisoned and killed.[10] On 13 September, the Ottoman parliament passed a law decreeing the 'expropriation and confiscation' of Armenian property, and Armenians began to be marched from Turkey to the Syrian town of Deir ez Zor. En route and subsequently in twenty-five concentration camps near Turkey's modern borders with Iraq and Syria, 1.5 million were killed. Some were killed in mass burnings, others by injection by morphine, yet others by toxic gas. It is a history that is not often told, and the genocide of the Armenians is clear proof (if any were needed) that the Holocaust was not unique to the Nazis.

Here's my last example of extreme human cruelty, this time from the Democratic Republic of Congo.[vi] Mirindi Euprazi was at home in her village of Ninja in the Walungu region in 1994 when the rebels attacked. She told her story:

'They forced my son to have sex with me, and when he'd finished they killed him. Then they raped me in front of my husband and then they killed him too. Then they took away my three daughters.'

She hasn't heard of the three girls since. She describes being left naked while her house was burned. I imagine – like me – you are astonished beyond words by this event. How do rebel soldiers lose sight of the fact that the person they raped is a woman, no different to their own mothers? How can they treat her as an object in this way? How do they ignore that this boy – forced to have sex with his mother – is just a teenager, with normal feelings?

But that's more than enough as examples of human cruelty from different cultures to remind us of what humans are capable. My claim is that low empathy is necessary but not sufficient for acts of cruelty. Necessary, because if empathy by definition prevents you from hurting another person, its absence makes hurting another person possible. But not sufficient because, as we shall see, low empathy merely sets the scene for cruelty – but it is not the only possible outcome. If I'm right that acts of cruelty are the result of no empathy, then what we need urgently are answers to the more basic questions of what is empathy, and why do some people have less than others?

2

The Empathy Mechanism:
The Bell Curve

Unempathic acts are simply the tail end of a bell curve, found in every population on the planet. If we want to replace the term 'evil' with the term 'empathy erosion', we have to understand empathy closely.

The key idea is that *we all lie somewhere on an empathy spectrum* (from high to low). People said to be 'evil' or cruel are simply at one extreme of the empathy spectrum. We can all be lined up along this spectrum of individual differences, based on how much empathy we have. In this chapter we begin the search to understand why some people have more or less empathy. We need to understand the empathy bell curve both to get underneath the surface of this mysterious, powerful substance, empathy, and because at one end of this spectrum we find 'zero degrees of empathy'.

But first we need a definition of empathy. There are lots of ways to define it but here's how mine begins:

> *Empathy occurs when we suspend our single-minded focus of attention, and instead adopt a double-minded focus of attention.*

'Single-minded' attention means we are thinking only about our *own* mind, our current thoughts or perceptions. 'Double-minded' attention means we are keeping in mind *someone else's* mind, *at the very same time*. This immediately gives a clue to what empathy entails. When empathy is switched off, we think only about our own interests. When empathy is switched on, we focus on other people's interests too. Sometimes attention is compared to a spotlight, so this new definition of empathy suggests our attention can either be a single spotlight (shining through the darkness on our own interests) or it can be accompanied by a second spotlight (shining on someone else's interests).

But the definition of empathy doesn't stop there. This first part of the definition merely delineates the form that empathy takes (the dual focus). It also hints at the kind of mechanism in the brain that empathy requires: a separation of how we reflect on two minds at once (self, and other).[vii] We're going to look at empathy in the brain later in this chapter. But so far my definition ignores the process and the content of what happens during empathy. So we can extend the definition of empathy as follows:

> *Empathy is our ability to identify what someone else is thinking or feeling, and to respond to their thoughts and feelings with an appropriate emotion.*

This suggests there are at least two stages in empathy: recognition and response. Both are needed, since if you have the former without the latter you haven't empathized at all. If I can see in your face that you are struggling to lift your suitcase onto the overhead rack on the train and I just sit there and watch, then I have failed to respond to your feelings (of frustration). Empathy therefore requires not only that you can *identify* another person's feelings and thoughts, but that you *respond* to these with an appropriate emotion too.[viii] Later in the book I'll be introducing you to people with particular medical conditions where one or both of these components of empathy are missing, or fail to develop normally.

When that second spotlight is working, and you are able to both recognize and respond, you can not only ask someone how they are feeling, you can sensitively avoid hurting their feelings, think about how to make them feel good, and consider how everything you say or do impacts on them or others. When they tell you how they are, you can follow up not just on what they say, but also on how they say it – reading their face as if it transparently reflects their inner thoughts and feelings. If they are suffering to any degree, you just *know* to offer comfort and sympathy.

But if your attention has a single focus – *your* current interest, goal, wish, or plan – with no reference to another person or their thoughts and feelings, then your empathy is effectively switched off. It might be switched off because your attention is elsewhere, a transient fluctuation in your state. For example, if you are rummaging frenetically through your belongings, your attention might be focused solely on your own current goal of urgently finding something. Some *thing*. At that moment, you may have lost sight of another person, or at least lost sight of *their* feelings. In such a state of single-mindedness, the other person – or their feelings – no longer exists. All that matters is solving your immediate problem: finding the object, fixing something, whatever it is you are trying to achieve. If someone interrupted you to ask what you were doing, your narrative would be one-sided: a report of your own current preoccupation. The language you would use to describe this state would be totally *self*-focused.

In this book we encounter people who are imprisoned in their own self-focus. Imprisoned, because for them it is not a temporary state of mind after which their empathy can recover. For them, self-focus is *all* that is available to them, as if a chip in their neural computer is missing. A temporary fluctuation in one's empathy is potentially rescuable. An enduring lack of empathy, as a stable trait, potentially is not.

Being able to empathize means being able to understand accurately the other person's position, to identify with 'where they are at'. It means being able to find solutions to what might otherwise be a deadlock between incompatible goals. Empathy makes the other person feel valued, enabling them to feel their thoughts and feelings have been heard, acknowledged and respected. Empathy allows you to make a close friend and to look after the friendship. Empathy avoids any risk of misunderstandings or miscommunication, by figuring out what the other person might have intended. It allows you to avoid causing offence by anticipating how things will be experienced by another mind, different to your own. Just because *you* thought your actions or words were harmless fun doesn't mean the other person will receive them in the same way. Although this book mostly focuses on the negative sides of too little empathy, it is vital to keep in mind these positive benefits of average – or even superior – levels of empathy.

My definition of empathy so far presumes it is either present or absent. When our attention lapses into single focus, empathy has been turned off. When we shift our attention to dual focus, empathy has been turned back on. This portrait of empathy is as a binary operation (off or on), like a light bulb in the head. In reality, empathy is more like a dimmer control than an all-or-none switch. In science, dimmer controls suggest a spectrum or a quantitative scale, from low to medium to high. On this quantitative view, empathy varies in the population. Now imagine we had a way of measuring empathy (there are such instruments, so this is not idle science fiction) so that you can assign everyone an empathy score. The result is the familiar bell-shaped curve or normal distribution, shown below.

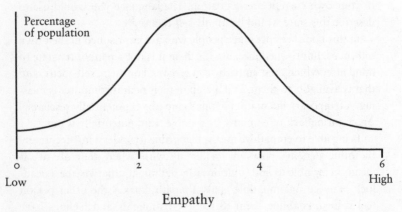

Figure 3: The empathy bell curve

In Figure 3 we see that some people are high in empathy, some medium, and some low. I will be arguing that some people are at the low end of this empathy dimension in a potentially permanent way, and that some (but importantly not all) of those at this extreme end are people who we might call 'evil' or cruel. That is, they never had much empathy and they may never. Others may be at the low end of the empathy dimension because they have experienced a transient shutting down of their empathy, as a result of their current situation. That is, they had empathy and lost it, however briefly. But, however you get to this low point on the empathy scale, the result can be the

14

same. In this sense, reduced empathy is the final common pathway that is necessary (but not sufficient) to cause cruelty. At that point, you become capable of dehumanizing other people, of turning the other person into an object, and this can have tragic consequences.

To turn to the key question of what determines whether you are high, medium or low in empathy, we need an empirical, scientific study of empathy. And the start of any empirical study is measurement.

MEASURING EMPATHY

As part of our research into the nature of empathy, my colleagues (Sally Wheelwright, Bonnie Auyeung and Carrie Allison) and I developed a scale with which to measure empathy across the age range. Working with this creative team was fun. We found that the main empathy test being used in psychological research was arguably *not* a pure measure of empathy,[ix] so we devised our own scale, called the Empathy Quotient (or EQ). We designed it to have questions related to each of the two main components of empathy (the recognition and the response). It works well in that it distinguishes people who have an empathy difficulty from those who do not.[12] Ten examples (out of forty) from the EQ are shown below (and you can find the full version in Appendix 1):

The Adult Version of the Empathy Quotient (EQ)

1. I can easily tell if someone else wants to enter a conversation.
2. I find it difficult to explain to others things that I understand easily, when they don't understand it first time.
3. I really enjoy caring for other people.
4. I find it hard to know what to do in a social situation.
5. People often tell me that I went too far in driving my point home in a discussion.
6. It doesn't bother me too much if I am late meeting a friend.
7. Friendships and relationships are just too difficult, so I tend not to bother with them.
8. I often find it difficult to judge if something is rude or polite.

9. In a conversation, I tend to focus on my own thoughts rather than on what my listener might be thinking.
10. When I was a child, I enjoyed cutting up worms to see what would happen.

If you agree with items 1 and 3, this would get you two EQ points. If you disagreed with item 2 and items 4–10, this would give you a total of ten EQ points. In this case, the higher your score, the better your empathy.

The adult version of the EQ depends on self-report. It works well in large samples of people and reveals, for example, that students working in the humanities score slightly higher on the EQ than students working in the sciences[13] and females in the general population score slightly higher on the EQ than males.[14] Most importantly, the EQ produces that empathy bell curve that we expected to find in the population.

Relying on self-report could be problematic, since a person might believe they are much more empathic than they really are. This is because someone with poor empathy is often the last person to realize they have poor empathy. It just goes with the territory: as you lose your empathy you may also lose your awareness that you have poor empathy. This is because built into the very nature of empathy is that double-mindedness. Double-mindedness can be used not just to think about how *others* feel or what they might be thinking, but also to think about how *you* may be perceived by others. Imagining yourself from another person's vantage point is what we mean by self-awareness. When I meet someone with very little empathy it is as if they lack the very apparatus to look inwards at themselves, as if they lack a reverse periscope that would enable any vision of him or herself.

Worries about whether some people might not fill in their EQ accurately are probably unimportant because when you have large samples of data, occasional inaccuracies are cancelled out. We went on to develop a child version of the EQ, filled in by the parent. Just as we found with the adult version of the EQ, we found that on average girls have a slightly higher EQ than boys.[15] (You can find these different versions of the EQ in Appendix 1). So the EQ enables us to visualize who is high, medium or low in empathy. We'll meet some extremely low scorers in the next chapter, but before that I want to give you some feel of the range of individual differences in EQ.

THE EMPATHIZING MECHANISM

Imagine there is a circuit in the brain – the empathy circuit – that determines how much empathy you have. Let's call it the Empathizing Mechanism. From the EQ we can discern that the Empathizing Mechanism has seven likely settings.[x] These are broad bands and we may move around a little within a band from one day to another, due to the transient fluctuations in our empathy. But which band we are in is broadly fixed.

At **Level 0**, an individual has no empathy at all. In Chapter 3 we meet individuals who are at this level and who wind up in clinics voluntarily seeking a diagnosis, or who have been compulsorily detained (as we say in England, 'at Her Majesty's pleasure') because they have got into trouble with the law, or who have had a diagnosis imposed on them. At Level 0 some people become capable of committing crimes, including murder, assault, torture and rape. Fortunately not all people at Level 0 do cruel things to others, since others at this level just find relationships very difficult but have no wish to harm others. For others at Level 0, even when it is pointed out to them that they have hurt another person, *this means nothing to them.* They cannot experience remorse or guilt because they just don't understand what the other person is feeling. This is the ultimate extreme: zero degrees of empathy.

At **Level 1**, the person may still be capable of hurting others, but they can reflect on what they have done to some extent and show regret. It's just that, at the time, they can't stop themselves. Clearly, empathy is not having a sufficient brake on their behaviour. For individuals at this level, a part of the brain's empathy circuit 'goes down' that would normally enable them to inhibit themselves from hurting others, physically. Under certain conditions the person may be able to show a degree of empathy, but if their violent temper is triggered the person may report that their judgement becomes completely clouded, or that they 'see red'. At that moment, other people's feelings are no longer on their radar. What is frightening is how this breakdown in the empathy circuit can leave the individual capable of extreme violence. At the moment of the assault, the urge to attack and destroy may be so overwhelming there are no limits to what the person could do and their victim is at that moment simply an object, to be vanquished or removed.

At **Level 2** a person still has major difficulties with empathy, but they have enough to have a glimmering of how another person would feel for this to inhibit any physical aggression. This may not stop them shouting at others, or saying hurtful things to others, but they have enough empathy to realize they have done something wrong when another person's feelings are hurt. However, they typically need the feedback from that person, or from a bystander, to realize that they have over-stepped the mark. Anticipating another person's feelings in subtle ways just does not come naturally to them. A person at Level 2 therefore blunders through life, saying all the wrong things (e.g., 'You've put on weight!') or doing the wrong things (e.g., invading another person's 'personal space'). They are constantly getting into trouble for these faux pas, at work or at home, perhaps losing their job or their friends because of it, yet are mystified as to what they are doing wrong.

At **Level 3** a person knows they have difficulty with empathy and may try to mask or compensate for this, perhaps avoiding jobs or relationships where there are constant demands on their empathy; making the effort to 'pretend to be normal'[16] can be exhausting and stressful. They may avoid others at work because social interaction is so hard, and just keep their head down and do their work in the hope that this doesn't bring them into contact with too many other people. They may realize they just don't understand jokes that everyone else does, that other people's facial expressions are hard to read, and that they are never quite sure what's expected of them. Small talk, chatting and conversation may be a nightmare for someone at this level, because there are no rules for how to do it and it is all so unpredictable. When they get home, the relief (that comes from no longer having to 'fake' being like everyone else) is huge: they just want to be alone, to be themselves.

At **Level 4**, a person has a 'low-average' amount of empathy. Most of the time their slightly blunted empathy does not affect their everyday behaviour, though people with this level of empathy may feel more comfortable when the conversation shifts to topics other than the emotions. More men than women are at Level 4, preferring to solve problems by doing something practical, or offering to fix something technical, rather than having prolonged discussions about feelings.[17] Friendships may be more based on shared activities and interests than on emotional intimacy, though are no less enjoyable or weaker because of this.

At **Level 5**, individuals are marginally above average in empathy, and more women than men are at this level. Here, friendships may be more based on emotional intimacy, sharing confidences, mutual support and expressions of compassion. While people at Level 5 are not constantly thinking about others' feelings, other people are nevertheless on their radar a lot of the time, such that they are far more careful in how they interact at work or at home. They hold back from asserting their opinion, so as not to dominate or intrude. They do not rush to make unilateral decisions so that they can consult and take into account a range of perspectives. They take their time with others even if they have lots of other things to do, because they want to find out (sensitively and indirectly) how the other person is and what's on their mind – information that is better gleaned by chatting around a range of topics, rather than being extracted by direct interrogation.

At **Level 6** we meet individuals with remarkable empathy, who are continuously focused on other people's feelings, and go out of their way to check on these and to be supportive. It is as if their empathy circuit is in a constant state of hyper-arousal, such that other people are never off their radar. Rather than try to describe this type, let me give you a sketch of one such person:

> Hannah is a psychotherapist who has a natural intuition in tuning into how others are feeling. As soon as you walk into her living room, she is already reading your face, your gait, your posture. The first thing she asks you is 'How *are* you?' but this is no perfunctory platitude. Her intonation – even before you have taken off your coat – suggests an invitation to confide, to disclose, to share. Even if you just answer with a short phrase, your tone of voice to her reveals your inner emotional state and she quickly follows up your answer with 'You sound a bit sad. What's happened to upset you?'
>
> Before you know it, you are opening up to this wonderful listener, who only interjects to offer *sounds* of comfort and concern, to mirror

how you feel, occasionally offering soothing words to boost you and make you feel valued. Hannah is not doing this because it is her job to do it. She is like this with her clients, her friends, and even with people she has only just met. Hannah's friends feel cared for by her, and her friendships are built around sharing confidences and mutual support. She has an unstoppable drive to empathize.[xi]

THE EMPATHY CIRCUIT

What leads an individual's Empathizing Mechanism to be set at different levels? The most immediate answer is that it depends on the functioning of a special circuit in the brain, the empathy circuit. In this section we take a tour of the empathy circuit, and in the next chapter we see how this circuit is under-active in those people who commit acts of cruelty, and in those who struggle to empathize.

Thanks to functional magnetic resonance imaging (fMRI), scientists are getting a clear picture of the brain areas that play a central role when we empathize. There is a consensus in neuroscience[18] that it is not the *whole* brain that is involved in empathy, but at least ten interconnected brain regions are involved (and more may await discovery). They are shown in Figure 4, and I'll take you through each of them briefly. The names of each of these regions in the empathy circuit can seem alien on first reading, but with a little familiarity they become like old friends! There have been some imaginative experiments using neuroimaging to reveal the different parts of the empathy circuit.

The first region in the empathy circuit is the **medial prefrontal cortex (MPFC)**, which is thought of as a 'hub' for social information processing and is important for comparing your own perspective to someone else's.[19-21] The MPFC divides into the dorsal part (dMPFC) and the ventral part (vMPFC). The dMPFC is involved in thinking about other people's thoughts and feelings[19, 22] (sometimes called 'meta-representation'), as well as when we think about our own thoughts and feelings.[20, 23] In contrast, the vMPFC is biased to being used when people think about their own mind more than someone else's – demonstrated by my talented former doctoral student Mike

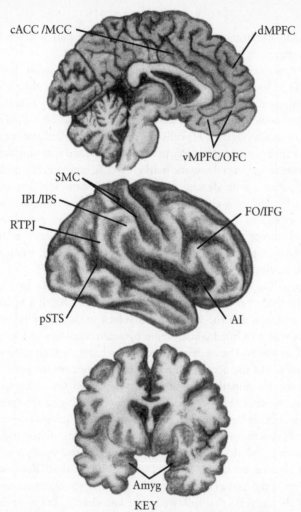

KEY

AI - anterior insula
Amyg – amygdala
cACC – caudal anterior cingulate cortex
dMPFC/vMPFC – dorsal/ventral medial prefrontal cortex
FO – frontal operculum
IFG – inferior frontal gyrus
IPL – inferior parietal lobule

IPS – inferior parietal sulcus
MCC – middle cingulate cortex
OFC – orbito-frontal cortex
pSTS – posterior superior temporal sulcus
RTPJ – right temporal-parietal junction
SMC – somatosensory cortex

Figure 4: Regions in the social brain (produced by Mike Lombardo, with thanks)

Lombardo. He argues that the vMPFC seems to play a key role in self-awareness.[20, 24–26]

But that's not all this brain region does. Neuroscientist Antonio Damasio at Iowa University put forward the theory that the vMPFC stores information about the emotional valence of a course of action. If an action is rewarding it is emotionally positive, while if it is punishing it is emotionally negative. He calls this a 'somatic marker' and suggests we have such a marker for every action we make, and that only actions with positively valenced somatic markers will be repeated. His evidence is that patients with damage in the vMPFC show less 'autonomic response'[26] (less of a change in their heart-beat, for example) when shown images of distressing scenes (like disasters and mutilations).[xii] Further evidence that the vMPFC marks 'emotional valence' is that it is involved in positive or optimistic thinking[27] and that, when their vMPFC is stimulated, depressed people feel less negative.[28]

Phineas Gage (1823–60) must be one of the most famous cases from the field of neuropsychology, and without realizing it he added to the evidence that the vMPFC is involved in the empathy circuit. Phineas was a railroad construction foreman who survived an accident of an iron rod being driven through his brain. Arguably, the main consequence of the accident (he lived for another twelve years) was that he lost his empathy.[xiii] Here's how it happened. On 13 September 1848, at the age of twenty-five, Phineas was working on the railroad, blasting rock in Vermont. His job was to add the gunpowder and a fuse and press the gunpowder down into a hole using an iron rod. The gunpowder exploded unexpectedly, driving the rod up through the side of his face, behind his left eye, and exiting his skull. Remarkably he sat up in the cart as they drove him to the hospital, conscious and talking. In the years that followed, the main change that was noticed was that, whereas previously Phineas had been a polite individual, now he was childish, irreverent and rude, uttering profanities and showing no social inhibition. He had lost his empathy.[xiv] More than a century later, neuroscientist Hanna Damasio and colleagues obtained his preserved skull and, using modern neuroimaging, calculated that the rod must have damaged his vMPFC.[29, 30, 32, 33] We'll see how the vMPFC, and other regions in the empathy circuit, are under-active in people with low empathy. But first we need to map the different parts of the circuit.

The vMPFC overlaps with what is sometimes called the **orbito-frontal cortex (OFC)**. Back in 1994 my colleague Howard Ring and I were the first to identify the OFC as part of the empathy circuit, in that we found that when people were asked to judge which words described what the mind could do, the OFC was specifically activated.[34] The word list contained words like *think*, *pretend* and *believe* as well as words like *jump*, *walk* and *eat*. Later my colleague Valerie Stone and I found that patients with damage in the OFC had difficulty judging when a faux pas had occurred, an indicator of difficulties with empathy.[35] Damage to the OFC can also lead to patients losing their social judgement, becoming socially 'disinhibited'. In addition, when you see a needle going into a normal (but not an anaesthetized) hand, the OFC is active, suggesting this part of the empathy circuit is involved in judging whether something is painful or not.[36]

Adjacent to this area is the **frontal operculum (FO)**, which is not only part of the empathy circuit but the language circuit too, since it contains an area involved in the expression of language. Damage to this area can therefore result in difficulties producing fluent speech (also called Broca's aphasia, where the person can understand sentences but not express themselves in full sentences). Its relevance to empathy though comes from the idea that the FO is equivalent to an area in the monkey brain involved in coding other animals' intentions and goals.[37] That is, when a monkey (with a deep electrode in its brain) sees *another* monkey reaching for an object, cells in the FO increase their electrical activity, and the same cells fire when the monkey reaches for an object for itself.

The FO sits above a larger area called the **inferior frontal gyrus (IFG)**. Damage to this region can produce difficulties in emotion recognition.[31] Another of my talented former PhD students, Bhismadev Chakrabarti, got people to fill in the Empathy Quotient (EQ) and then had them lie still in a brain scanner while they looked at different facial expressions. Some examples of the faces they had to look at are shown in Figure 5. Bhisma had a hunch that the IFG would play a key role in empathy, and it was a very testable hypothesis. To test this,

Bhisma used the fMRI scanner to establish which brain regions responded to each of four 'basic' emotions (happy, sad, angry and disgust).

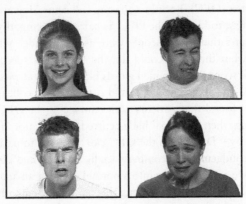

Figure 5: Examples of happy, sad, angry and disgusted faces

I always smile when I see these images because the one at the top left is my daughter Kate when she was just nine years old. (She's meant to be looking happy, which can't really be said of the other three.) Bhisma found that disgust is mostly processed in the anterior insula (AI), happy is mostly processed in the ventral striatum, anger in the supplementary motor cortex, and sad in a number of regions, including the hypothalamus.[38, 39] He then looked to see if there was any region in the brain that consistently correlated with EQ, regardless of the emotion the person was viewing. The IFG fitted the bill. The better your empathy, the more active your IFG, when looking at emotional faces.

Going deeper into the cortex we find the **caudal anterior cingulate cortex (cACC)**, also called the **middle cingulate cortex (MCC)**. The cACC/MCC is involved in empathy because it is activated as part of the 'pain matrix'. This region is not only active when you experience pain but also when you are observing others in pain.[40] Then we come to the **anterior insula (AI)** that has been identified as playing a role in bodily aspects of self-awareness, itself closely tied to empathy (as we discussed earlier).[41] Zurich neuroscientist Tania Singer and her colleagues used fMRI and found that when a person received a painful stimulus on their own hand or their partner's hand, the AI and the cACC/MCC are activated whether you are experiencing your own pain or perceiving your loved one's pain.[42] Chicago neuroscientist Jean Decety and colleagues also showed that if you watch someone's hand being caught in a door, the AI and cACC/MCC are also activated.[43] This activation is modulated by the extent that you are imagining yourself as that other person.[44] The AI is also active when you experience a disgusting taste or see someone else showing disgust, again suggesting this is the part of the brain that allows identification with another person's emotional state.[45]

Tania Singer also looked at the brain when you are judging if a person is playing fairly. She found that both men and women activate their cACC/MCC and AI when they see someone in pain who they regard as fair and someone they like. Interestingly, men on average show less activity in this part of the empathy circuit when they see someone in pain who they regard as unfair or who they do not like.[46] It is as if men find it easier to switch off their empathy for those who might be competitors, or who they judge are out of line, or with whom they have no vested interest in remaining in a relationship. The cACC/MCC and AI are also clearly involved in the experience and recognition of a range of emotions, from happiness to disgust and pain,[42, 45, 47-49] and damage to these regions can interfere with the ability to recognize such emotions. For all these reasons, these are key parts of the empathy circuit.

The **temporo-parietal junction** on the right side (**RTPJ**) has been found to play a key role in empathy, particularly when judging someone else's intentions and beliefs.[50] This is more relevant to the recognition element of empathy, or what is sometimes called a 'theory of mind'. We use our theory of mind when we try to imagine someone else's thoughts. Damage to the TPJ can lead not only to difficulties in judging someone's intentions but also to 'out of body' experiences[51] while stimulation of the RTPJ can give you the eerie experience that someone else is present when there is no one else with you.[52] These abnormalities suggest the RTPJ is involved in self-monitoring and monitoring others, though it may also be involved in non-social functions too (such as attention-switching).[53, 54]

Adjacent to the RTPJ is the **posterior superior temporal sulcus** (pSTS), which has been linked to the empathy circuit for many years, since animal research reveals that cells in the STS respond when the animal is monitoring the direction of someone else's gaze. In addition, damage to the STS can disrupt a person's ability to judge where some-one else is looking.[55] Clearly, we look at another person's eyes not just to see *where* they are looking but what they might be *feeling* about what they are looking at.[56] The STS is also involved when you observe 'biological motion' (animate, self-propelled kinds of movements that living creatures make).[57]

Next up in the empathy circuit is the **somatosensory cortex (SMC)**, which is not only involved in coding when you are having a tactile experience, but is also activated just by observing others being touched.[58–62, xv] In addition to being involved in sensory experience (as its name suggests), when you watch a needle piercing someone else's hand you get a burst of electrical activity in the somatosensory cortex,[xvi] and this is also seen using fMRI.[44, 64] This strongly suggests that we react in a very sensory way when we *identify* with someone else's distress. This clear brain response is telling us that even without any conscious decision to do so we must be putting ourselves into the other person's shoes, not just to imagine how we would feel in their situation, but actually feeling it as if it had been our *own* sensation. No wonder we wince involuntarily when we see someone else get hurt. Of course, not everyone will have this strong empathic response to such emotionally charged situations. If our somatosensory cortex is damaged or temporary disrupted, our ability to recognize other people's emotions is significantly diminished.[65, 66] Surgeons may, for example, be well suited to their job precisely because they don't have this emotional reaction, a prediction that was confirmed by Yawei Cheng who found that physicians who practise acupuncture show less somatosensory cortex activity while watching pictures of body parts being pricked by needles.[67]

The FO/IFG connects to the **inferior parietal lobule (IPL)** and these are both interesting because they are part of the 'mirror neuron system', those parts of the brain that are active when you perform an action and when you observe someone else performing the same action. Italian neuroscientists led by Giacomo Rizzolatti at the University of Parma first demonstrated the existence of mirror neurons in primates[68] by placing electrodes into parts of the brain to record nerve cells that fire not only when the animal is performing an action but also when the animal sees another animal performing the same action. If the IFG is part of the human mirror neuron system, this suggests empathy involves some form of mirroring of other people's actions and emotions.[47, 69] The mirror neuron system in humans is hard to measure, obviously because it is unethical to place electrodes into the awake human healthy brain.[xvii] But (using fMRI) the mirror neuron system appears to span the IFG, IPL and the **inferior parietal sulcus (IPS)** (just behind the IPL). Interestingly, an extension of this idea of a 'mirror neuron' is neurons that fire to direction of gaze. IPS neurons in a monkey not only fire when a monkey looks in a specific direction, but also when seeing another person (or monkey) looking in that same direction.[71]

As an aside, some people are quick to assume that mirror neurons alone can be equated with empathy, but we should keep in mind that the mirror neuron system has only been verified in single cell recordings for the domain of actions and may simply be building blocks for empathy. For example, the mirror neuron system is involved in *mimicry*, as happens when we are feeding an infant and, as they open their mouth, we involuntarily open our own; or as happens when someone else yawns and we involuntarily do too. Such mirroring of another's actions typically occurs without consciously thinking about the other person's emotional state. This effect is what some social psychologists call 'the chameleon effect'.[72] Equally, it has been suggested that *emotional contagion* is a form of empathy, as happens when one person shows fear and others (witnessing their facial expression) 'catch' the same feeling of fear; or when one baby cries in a maternity ward, triggering other babies to start crying. Again, one can imagine this type of 'contagion' happening without needing to think consciously about another's feelings. As I indicated earlier in the chapter, I reserve the term 'empathy' for more than these rather simple phenomena. Empathy seems to be more than just this automatic mirroring. Both the 'automatic' mirroring systems and the more 'conscious' neural systems involved in explicit understanding of mental states, emotions, and how others are related to oneself, interact with each other.[24, 73, 74]

The last region (but in many ways the jewel in the crown) in the empathy circuit is the **amygdala,** situated beneath the cortex in the 'limbic system'. It is involved in emotional learning and regulation processing.[75, 76] University of New York neuroscientist Joseph LeDoux situates the amygdala at the centre of 'the emotional brain'[77] because of his extensive studies in relation to how we learn to fear something.[xviii] (His fascination with the amygdala and his love of music prompted him to form a band called The Amygdaloids![xix]) I had the pleasure of meeting Joe when he visited Cambridge in 2009. A key piece of evidence for the role of the amygdala in empathy came from a study we carried out back in 1999, when we asked people whilst lying in the fMRI scanner to look at pictures of other people's eyes to make judgements about their emotions and mental states. One brain region that was clearly activated was the amygdala.[80] Another clue that the amygdala is part of the empathy circuit comes from a famous neurological patient, known by her initials, S. M. She has very specific damage to both of her two amygdalae (we all have one in each hemisphere). Despite having good intelligence, her main difficulty is not being able to recognize fearful emotions in others' faces.[81] This difficulty S. M. has in recognizing fearful faces is related to the fact that the eyes are critical for recognizing fear in someone's face. S. M.'s damage in the amygdala affects her ability to make eye contact, which is why she has difficulty recognizing fearful faces.[82] We know this because, when directed to attend to the eyes, she regains the ability to recognize fearful faces.[83] S. M. reminds us how key the amygdala is in cueing us to attend to the eyes, which gives us clues to other people's thoughts and emotions.

This completes our brief tour of the ten major brain regions involved in empathy.[xx] Many of the regions involved in automatically coding our own experience are also automatically active when we perceive others acting or having similar experiences.[xxi] Similarly, the regions involved in consciously thinking about someone else's mind are also active when thinking about our own mind.[xxii] These regions allow us to talk about an empathy circuit in the brain. As a circuit, these ten waystations are not connected in any simple linear fashion (like a string of pearls in a necklace), since there are multiple connections between regions too. Finding that these regions vary in activity in different individuals according to the person's particular level of empathy[73] takes us back to the idea of empathy varying like a dimmer control, and gives us a direct way of explaining people who have little or no empathy. What we should expect is that someone who is way down the empathy bell curve should show far *less* neural activity in parts or all of the empathy circuit. We'll be looking at precisely this prediction shortly.

So have we got any closer to explaining how people can be cruel to others? Can we now replace the term 'evil' with the term 'empathy'? Not yet. So far all we have is some evidence that people can score very low on the EQ, and we now have a list of brain regions whose functioning determines how much empathy a person will show. But this is not yet a satisfying explanation for several reasons. First, we need proof that these regions 'go down' in people who commit acts of cruelty towards others. Second, we need a clearer portrait of what people are like who score super-low on the EQ. Third, we need to know if there are different routes to arriving at zero degrees of empathy. And, lastly, we need to know what the environmental or biological factors are that can cause the empathy circuit in the brain to malfunction. If we can explain how this happens, we will have solved our quest to explain the extremes of human cruelty.

3

When Zero Degrees of
Empathy is Negative

What is *zero degrees of empathy* like? What does it mean to have no empathy? And does this translate into what some people call 'evil'?

Zero degrees of empathy means you have no awareness of how you come across to others, how to interact with others, or how to anticipate their feelings or reactions. Your Empathy Mechanism functions at Level 0. It leaves you feeling mystified by why relationships don't work out, and it creates a deep-seated self-centredness. Other people's thoughts and feelings are just off your radar. It leaves you doomed to do your own thing, in your own little bubble, not just oblivious of other people's feelings and thoughts but oblivious to the idea that there might even *be* other points of view. The consequence is that you believe 100 per cent in the rightness of your own ideas and beliefs, and judge anyone who does not hold your beliefs as wrong, or stupid.

Having zero degrees of empathy is ultimately a lonely kind of existence, a life at best misunderstood, at worst condemned as selfish. It means you have no brakes on your behaviour, leaving you free to pursue any object of your desires, or to express any thought in your mind, without considering the impact of your actions or words on another person. In the extreme case, it might lead you to commit murder or rape. In the less extreme case (close to zero, such as Level 1 or 2) it might lead you to be verbally abusive, or just to talk way too much, or to overstay your welcome. These are clearly different levels of empathy deficit, since the person who is simply verbally insensitive may realize it's not nice to physically hurt someone else. But even the verbally insensitive individual can be close to zero on the EQ. Zero degrees of empathy can lead one to commit acts of cruelty, or it can leave one insensitive to others, or it can leave one simply socially isolated. This underlines that zero degrees of empathy does *not* equate to what some would call 'evil'. But for those who come into the orbit of someone with such depleted empathy it means the risk of being on the receiving end of verbal insults, physical attacks, or experiencing a lack of care or consideration – in short, at risk of getting hurt.

Zero degrees of empathy does not strike at random in the population. There are at least three well-defined medical routes (and many non-medical routes) to getting to this end-point. In this chapter I put forward a new view where I take old categories from psychiatry and reconceptualize them as examples of zero degrees of empathy. I group these as Zero-Negative because they are unequivocally bad for the sufferer and for those around them. As we meet each of these, and

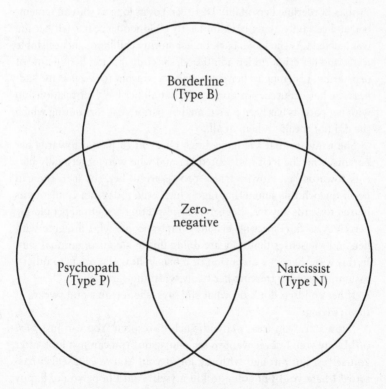

Figure 6: Three forms of Zero-Negative

look at their brains, we can see if it really is the case that, however you lose your empathy, if you are Zero-Negative the same underlying empathy circuitry in the brain is affected.

We are slowly going to look into each of the three circles shown in Figure 6, but we need to go one step at a time. The first form of Zero-Negative is called borderline (or Type B).

CAROL: ZERO-NEGATIVE TYPE B

Carol is thirty-nine years old. I met her when she came to our diagnostic clinic in Cambridge. (I have disguised details of her life for reasons of confidentiality.) She is classed as *borderline*. To give it its full name, she has Borderline Personality Disorder. For as long as she can remember, and certainly going back into early childhood, she has felt her life was 'cursed'. As she looks back on her stormy childhood, her unstable teens, and her crisis-ridden adulthood, she contemplates her lifetime of depression. Listening to her story makes you want to weep at the sadness she has endured, not just briefly, but all her life. Her relationship with her parents has been punctuated by periods of years during which she did not speak to them at all.

She is aware that she has a huge reservoir of hatred towards her parents, who she feels maltreated her and who were never really parents towards her. However nice people are to her, she feels she can never quench this simmering rage which even today can come out as hatred towards anyone she feels is disrespecting her. Often people she perceives as disrespecting her are simply people who disagree with her, and she senses that they are doing this in a confrontational way. In this way, there is a distortion or a bias in how she reacts to others, assuming they are treating her badly when they are not.

If her children don't do what she says, she screams and swears at them, saying:

'How *dare* you treat me with such disrespect? You can just *fuck off*! I *hate* you. I never want to see you again. You can just look after yourselves. I'm through with the lot of you! You're evil, selfish bastards! I hate you! I'm going to kill myself! And I hope you're happy knowing *you* made me do it!'

She will then storm out, slamming the door behind her.

Minutes later, she will drive to one of her friends and spend the evening having fun, leaving her children reeling with the impact of her hurtful words. When her hatred and anger bubble up, there is no chance of her stopping it coming out. It bursts forth with venom, designed to hurt whoever's ears the words land on. Her own feelings are so strong that there is no space in her mind to consider how her children might feel, being told by their mother that they are evil. The irony of Carol's behaviour is that, in accusing others of selfishness (because their will does not accord with hers), she herself behaves with absolute selfishness. Looking at Carol, we see a tragic figure: a woman who feels so hurt by others that at this point in her life, she is easily provoked into hurting others. Her actions are like non-verbal statements: Why should I care about your feelings when no one cares about mine?

If parenthood is defined by being able to put your own needs *second* to those of your child, she is ill equipped for parenthood. For Carol, her own needs are paramount and her children's needs (or anyone else's for that matter) hardly even feature on her radar. While her children are recovering from the bruising impact of her outburst, she is meantime laughing and partying with her friends in a café in town. When she comes back home, she either acts as if nothing has happened or refuses to talk to her children (or whoever provoked her rage) until they have apologized to her.

Hate and anger are not Carol's only problems. She also has major difficulties in interpreting other people's behaviour and emotional expressions (in their face, voice or gestures). She *thinks* she knows exactly what others are thinking or feeling, but her empathy is twisted and distorted by a bias which leads her to assume other people are thinking hostile thoughts and harbouring hostile intentions towards her. If someone is silent, even for a few minutes, she assumes they are being aggressive. If someone makes a joke, she assumes the other person is attacking her. If someone is caring, she assumes it is not meant. If someone apologizes, she assumes this too is not genuine. She will lash out with her accusations at other people's insincerity so that, no matter how hard they try to persuade her that they care or are sorry for their apparently hurtful actions, she does not accept their well-intended approaches and pushes them away. The fact that other people feel bullied and controlled by her tyrannical, self-centred behaviour does not even occur to her.

Carol is extremely difficult because her behaviour is so impulsive and explosive, but at the same time she also carves an extremely sad figure: At an age – thirty-nine – when she should feel confident and a sense of achievement with her efforts, she has instead ended up feeling distrustful of close relationships, constantly disappointed by others, and believing she has been victimized by others. To those who know Carol, her emotions are like a rollercoaster. She lurches from feeling lonely and depressed, to feeling totally happy, to feeling rage towards others. When she is not in the grip of one of these outbursts or crises, she can empathize, but her capacity to empathize is fragile, easily derailed by her own powerful feelings of feeling threatened that lurk just beneath the surface, ready to make her launch an attack on whoever she feels is the threat. As such, her capacity to empathize is highly unstable, just as is her mood. She goes out to clubs at night, dancing with strangers in the hope of finding a new close relationship. Some of these closer relationships develop into sexual relationships. She enjoys the idea that others find her attractive, and wants to feel close to someone. However, as soon as she is in a relationship she starts to sabotage it by initiating conflict. She will look for problems in the relationship, constantly asking 'Why don't you communicate?' and 'Why don't you care about me?'

Despite her latest lover, John, trying to reassure her that he does care, or replying that he does communicate, Carol will insist that he does not. When John gives her time to sit and talk, she argues that it is not 'real' communication. If he tries to defend himself, she accuses him of being 'switched off' or 'not really connecting with my pain'. She says that if he truly loved her, he would know how much she was hurting inside. She insists that he hates her, and taunts him to hit her, to prove that he hates her. After she has screamed at him and sworn at him, she will throw her arms around him and ask him to make love to her, begging him to 'promise me you'll never leave me!'

She frequently threatens to kill herself. On the last occasion, she ran outside at 3 a.m., claiming that John didn't care enough about her, and that 'this time I am going to do it'. He spent hours that night searching the local public parks, desolate car parks, waste land or other places where in the past she has run off to, to try to find her and console her and ask her to come back. Unsurprisingly, these unstable relationships tend not to last.

Within her marriage, she poured scorn on her husband, Mike, who she accused of making her feel insignificant, unimportant and invisible, as if she did not exist. When he replied that she does matter, she said, 'You're just like everyone else. You'll leave me in the end, just like everyone else does.' If Mike tried to comfort her by putting his arm around her, she pushed him away, saying he was suffocating her. She hates men touching her and does not want to be a wife, fearing it will take over her identity. She pushes away anyone who wants to get near her.

She is frequently totally self-absorbed, talking unstoppably about herself and her thoughts, with no real interest in other people's thoughts. If in bed her lover touches her, she removes his hand and tells him not to cross the midline of their bed. She tells him, 'You think you're so *fucking* important, just because you're at the top of the tree.' She says to him that in his presence she feels she is 'a nobody', and that he makes her feel like she is a 'piece of shit' and that the world would be better off if she was dead. She says she longs to be free of this life of pain, and that one of these days she will 'do it'. If John withdraws from her she hurls abuse at him, saying 'There! I told you you didn't care about me!' If he tries to get close to her, she tells him to 'go away and leave me alone. You don't really care about me.'

It is not hard to see why this is a clear case of Zero-Negative. Carol's empathy is at ground zero, and there is nothing good about being in such a state. She has few friends, a situation not helped by the fact that she despises other women. When she is alone she says she feels 'abandoned' and feels terrible levels of anxiety she can get rid of only through comfort eating, sex, alcohol, or aggression. One cannot help but feel compassion for her evident suffering. She can act as a mature woman one minute, and the next she can shift dramatically into being curled up like a little girl. She can appear calm and reflective, and then the next minute she can be highly manipulative ('Do this or else I'll take you to court . . .!'). One minute she can slam her friend's door, saying 'I'm never coming back', only to return the next week as if nothing had happened. She treats her few friends in the same hot and cold manner: one minute she tells them they are her *best* friend, the next minute she accuses them of disloyalty, claiming the friendship is false, and that they are *evil*.

This gives you a snapshot of Carol's current behaviour. The hall-mark of borderlines is a constant fear of abandonment, emotional pain and loneliness, hatred (of others, and of themselves), impulsivity and self-destructive, highly inconsistent behaviour. Jerold Kreisman and Hal Straus[90] summarize borderlines in the title of their book – *I Hate You, Don't Leave Me*. This neatly sums up the contradictory behaviour in borderlines. They are individuals who simultaneously need to lash out in what they perceive as self-protection, all the while craving others to offer them comfort and love. It is a heart-breaking combination.

So how did Carol end up as Zero-Negative? What is the route to becoming borderline? And does being borderline mean you inevitable treat people cruelly?

Carol's development

When Carol was a baby, her mother used to ignore her. She thought it would just spoil children to give them attention, that to show them affection was to 'make a rod for your back', by which she meant that the child would then expect love and become clingy. She breastfed Carol for just one week after she was born, and then passed the baby to a nanny to feed by bottle, saying she was too busy to look after the baby. She felt she had done her duty as a mother to have breastfed, but she got no maternal pleasure from such physical intimacy. She was proud of how Carol as a toddler showed independence, could be left alone for hours, or even all day, and did not cry, and she prided herself in having trained Carol to learn that crying did not bring her mother or lead to being picked up and cuddled. 'Children have to learn who is boss', she would say.

Carol was hit constantly if she didn't do what her mother ordered her to do. Carol can remember in her childhood frequently being sent from the table if her table manners were not to her mother's stand-ards, and her mother would then say, 'bread and water only, and stay in your room for a whole day'. If Carol cried at one of her punishments, she was threatened with being beaten with a belt, which her mother also used with the pet dog to control him. As we shall see, the link between borderline personality disorder and early abuse and neglect is very strong, leading to the view that borderlines in fact suffer from untreated form of childhood post-traumatic stress disorder. On this view, borderlines – even when they lash out at others – are themselves victims of early abuse. Carol recalls her mother showed no maternal affection, would never hug or kiss Carol, and constantly put her down, using criticism in public. She overtly favoured Carol's younger sister. At the age of eight, Carol was sent to boarding school, where she felt lonely and was withdrawn and socially anxious. Her mother felt she had completed her maternal duty and that children needed to learn to stand on their own two feet. As a result, Carol grew up looking after herself from at least the age of eight, if not before, knowing that her mother was never around to care for her. Clinicians call this precocious independence. She taught herself to read and figured out how to use the washing machine and clean the house, because her mother never did anything domestic. She would cook her own meals, clean the house, and cry herself to sleep every night.

Carol remembers her father being at times affectionate but also depressed, often away for long periods, his love unpredictable. She remembers the physical fights her parents had, while she would hide under her bed and block out the world with her fingers in her ears. This image powerfully sums up the view of borderlines as a child-as-victim. Carol's parents divorced when she was nine, and during her adolescence she hardly came home. When she wasn't at boarding school she would stay with friends, or come home to an empty home, as her mother was always out. She started having sexual relationships early, aged fourteen, in a desperate attempt to be loved. She turned to drugs, initially cannabis, but later 'acid', to escape her depression, and remembers how every day in her childhood she wished she could die, feeling that life was a struggle from which she wished she could exit.

When Carol was sixteen she was sitting in a café one day. She befriended a man in his forties who was sitting alone, and started pouring out her life story to him. He in turn told her of his difficult marriage, and his depression, and he asked her to be his friend. She identified with his sadness, and was flattered at being wanted by him.

He asked if she would come back to his apartment that evening to check a letter he was writing to his wife, and she willingly agreed. When she arrived later that evening he locked the door behind her and said how beautiful she was, and asked her to go to bed with him. She was frightened and did not want to, but said nothing while he had sex with her. After it was all over she felt she had been raped and that she had been being treated 'like dirt', but told no one. She felt as if this was what her life was destined to be like – she described it as 'her curse'.

At the age of eighteen she started cutting herself to escape her depression, drinking before going to clubs, and was surprised at how she couldn't remember how she ended up in different men's beds. After one such sexual encounter she became pregnant. She decided to keep the baby but developed post-natal depression when the baby was born. Her baby was taken into care, as she was unable to look after her. Four years later she married Mike, a man who offered to look after her, and had two more children with him, though the relationship – if it was ever there – did not last beyond a few short years. She soon simply used Mike to pay the bills, look after the children, and look after her, while she went out most nights clubbing. Her friendships are short-lived and are based on what she can get out of them. She doesn't want to hear about other people's problems. Often, all she cares about is herself.

Stepping back from Carol

Carol had a terrible childhood and adolescence. More than a century of research into the effects of early deprivation has clearly established that such environmental factors affect brain development, probably irreversibly. We need to ask: what makes us say she is borderline (or Type B)? And what are the consequences for behaviour in someone who is borderline?

According to psychiatrists, borderline is a highly specific form of personality disorder, different to other varieties. Borderlines, it turns out, are pretty common: they make up around 2 per cent of the general population. Among those who turn up for counselling or psychiatric help, it is even more common: about 15 per cent are borderline. Among people who commit suicide, about a third are borderline. And if you look in clinics for those with eating disorders, alcoholism and drug abuse, Type B may be present in as many as 50 per cent.[91-93]

The hallmarks of borderlines are self-destructive impulsivity, anger and mood swings. (You can see the list of 'symptoms' for borderlines in Appendix 2.) It is for this reason that there is a discussion among the psychiatric community to rename borderline personality disorder to be 'emotional dysregulation disorder' or 'emotionally impulsive personality disorder'. Borderlines also tend to think in very black and white ways (so-called 'splitting'), so that people are 'all good' or 'all bad'. (This may be why borderlines can be particularly attracted to cults, as the cult leader is seen as all good.) Borderlines are also very manipulative, for example acting as if they are weak and helpless, or using sexual seduction, or threatening suicide to get attention. From their point of view, this is not done to be cruel: it is an act of desperation to get what they crave, the attention and love they feel they never got as a child. In terms of the two major components of empathy (recognition and response) it may be that Type Bs have difficulties in both – they are certainly failing to *react* to others with an appropriate emotion,[341] and it may be they also have difficulty *reading* intentions and emotions in faces accurately.

Among borderlines in clinics, 70 per cent have attempted suicide before arriving in the clinic, and on average borderline patients attempt suicide at least three times in their life. For this reason, borderlines are said to have 'the most lethal psychiatric disorder'.[94-98] Distinguishing between those who 'merely' threaten suicide to get attention (but have no intention of carrying it out) versus those who actually plan to carry it out can be tricky. About 10 per cent of borderlines actually commit suicide, while the other 90 per cent just threaten or attempt it. Threatening to commit suicide is clearly not an empathic thing to do to another person. Whether the 10 per cent who succeed actually meant to succeed is also unclear, since it could just have been an attention-seeking impulse that went disastrously wrong. But it leaves others in a quandary: if your partner or relative threatens suicide, do you just dismiss it as attention seeking and ignore it? Or do you get swept up into the panic and the emergency of the situation, just in case this time he or she really means it?[99]

Borderlines *rage* towards those they love. When people say it is a thin line between love and hate, in borderlines that thin line becomes infinitesimal! Despite all this rage, they describe themselves as 'empty' inside. They will tell you quite openly that the empty feelings cause a terrible emotional pain and depression. And they will tell you that the impulsive behaviour (the drinking, drugs, self-mutilation, sexual prom-iscuity, binge eating, gambling or suicidal attempts) are all just to get some brief relief, a desperate attempt to feel something, anything, rather than feel the emptiness. No wonder one website for borderlines is called www.anythingtostopthepain.com

Borderlines also tell you that that feeling of emptiness leaves them with a lack of core identity. Life feels like an act, as if they are con-tinuously pretending to be someone else. And in the same way that deep down they don't know who they are, they also find it difficult to figure out who other people are. It is as if the problem they have in thinking about themselves mirrors the problem they have thinking about others as whole people. Instead, they focus either on the good parts of others, or their bad parts; they cannot seem to see a person as both good *and* bad. Those they love can switch from being perceived as perfect to being perceived as evil, even in minutes. People are either idolized, or devalued. This 'splitting' is sometimes thought of as a Freudian defence mechanism, though another view is as a sign of a mind that thinks in a very binary way; there are no shades of grey.

Marilyn Monroe

A well-known borderline was Marilyn Monroe (baptised Norma Jeane Baker). Despite her glamorous outward appearance, a volcano simmered within her. Elton John wrote his famous song 'Candle in the Wind' to describe her, which succinctly summarizes how impulsively changeable she was. Norma was born in 1926 and her parents divorced in 1928. She always claimed she didn't know who her real father was. Norma's mother Gladys, because of her mental health, gave her away for fostering to the Bolender family, where she lived until she was seven. Norma believed the Bolenders were her real parents until she was told the truth at this age. Gladys came back into her life and her daughter went to live with her again, but after Gladys was admitted to a psychiatric hospital, her mother's friend Grace became Norma's guardian. Grace married a man called Ervin Goddard when Norma was nine years old, so the young Norma was sent to the Los Angeles Orphan Home and a series of foster homes. Two years later she went back to live with Grace but was sexually molested by Goddard.

Norma was married three times, first to neighbour James Dougherty in 1942 when she was sixteen years old. He agreed to marry her to avoid her being returned to the orphanage. The marriage lasted only three years. She remarried in 1954, to baseball player Joe DiMaggio, but this time the marriage lasted less than a year. Very soon after, in 1956, she married playwright Arthur Miller, who described her as follows: 'She was a whirling light to me then, all paradox and enticing mystery, street-tough one moment, then lifted by a lyrical and poetic sensitivity that few retain past early adolescence.'[100] Throughout her life she hated being alone, and was terrified of being abandoned. In adulthood she was in and out of psychiatric clinics, and attempted suicide at least three times. Tragically, she finally succeeded in killing herself (overdosing on barbiturates) on 5 August 1962.

But let's return to our main objective here: to understand this form of zero degrees of empathy. As we heard in both Carol's case and Marilyn Monroe's life, borderlines cannot tolerate being alone. For them, aloneness feels like abandonment, and to avoid that awful feeling the person will seek out other people, even relationships with strangers. But, whoever they are with, borderlines either feel suffocated (by someone getting close to them) or abandoned (by someone being distant from them). They cannot find a calm middle ground in which to enjoy a relationship comfortably. Instead they go through an unhealthy alternating sequence of pushing others away (with angry hate), or clinging desperately to them (with extreme gratitude).

Borderlines were first described in 1938 by Adolf Stern, who saw the condition as *borderline* between psychosis and neurosis (a mild form of schizophrenia). We now know it is really very different to schizophrenia, but what is known about its cause?

Blame the parents

One of the earliest child psychological theories of borderlines was Object Relations Theory. This argued that, if parents don't respect their child's needs, or abuse or neglect their child, the child will become borderline. Object Relations Theory stems from four important psychodynamic ideas.

The first is that of the 'significant other' (typically a parent), who is the 'object' of a child's feelings, and to whom the child looks to meet his or her needs. The second is Freud's notion of stages of development that a child has to successfully negotiate to establish a healthy personality. The third is the Freudian principle of the importance of the earliest relationship influencing all later ones. The fourth idea (stemming back to Hungarian-born New York psychoanalyst Margaret Mahler) is that typical infants start in an 'autistic phase' of development, where they feel fused with their mother, and then later separate and individuate. During this 'separation-individuation phase', the child establishes their sense of self, crucial for later mental health. This process balances the healthy needs for autonomy and for closeness on the one hand, and the unhealthy fear of 'engulfment' and abandonment on the other.

Otto Kernberg developed these ideas into an explanation of borderlines. He is a professor of psychiatry at Weill Cornell Medical College and Director of the Personality Disorders Institute at the college, and was born in 1928 in Vienna.[xxiii] Like Mahler, Kernberg believed infants start off in an autistic state and have to build their first relationship, out of which comes a concept of self. During the phase of separating and individuating, the typical child uses a defence mechanism known as 'splitting'. Good experiences are split off from bad ones. For Kernberg, the natural process of development is to be able to integrate these splits both into accepting the self as comprising good and bad parts, and into accepting the parent as having both good and bad parts.

In Kernberg's account, a child who gets stuck at the splitting stage and who never achieves that integration enters into a 'dissociative' state and is destined to become borderline. It could be because the mother frequently pushed her child away or provided no closeness, or the mother may have made it hard for the child to explore the world by clinging too much to her infant. Therefore the child feared he would be abandoned (if she let go) or engulfed (by her holding him too much). Or a dissociative state could be as a result of more extreme deprivation or maltreatment, such as child abuse. The result is a child who never achieves a sense of being an emotionally secure adult. Being stuck with the split, the good experiences and the good image the child has of the parent can be amplified or exaggerated into idealization of the other and a grandiose view of oneself, while the bad experiences are quarantined into a cesspit of negative feelings (anger and hate). The result is an intense need for attachment, an intense fear of abandonment, and a conflict-ridden relationship with the mother.

So much for Object Relations Theory. It is a clever theory, because it makes sense of some central characteristics of borderlines, such as the black and white thinking style and the switching that can occur from extreme love to extreme hate. However, many of its predictions about parenting are quite subtle for scientists to measure. How much is too much – or how little is too little – when it comes to hugging your toddler? And it suffers, like many theories of its day, from a bias towards 'mother-blaming' that neglects other potential environmental factors (including abusive fathers, step-parents or others in the caregiver role).

An easier way to test Object Relations Theory is to take the clearcut cases of child physical abuse (when children are identified as having been battered, for example) or child sexual abuse, or child neglect (when children are identified as having been left alone for unusually long periods). When you look at children who have had such experiences, and follow them up, certainly there is plenty of evidence for a link with becoming borderline in adulthood.[101, 102] Common within families of children who later grow up to become borderline are incest, child abuse, violence and alcoholism. Obviously, the link between child abuse and becoming borderline is not total: not all who are abused go on to become borderline, and not all those who are borderline were abused. In fact, 80 per cent of those with a history of sexual abuse are not borderline.[103–110] Nevertheless, the link is strong. Between 40 and 70 per cent of borderlines report a history of sex abuse.[105] Between 60 and 80 per cent of borderlines also had a history of physical abuse, or early parental separation through divorce, or emotional neglect, indifference, deprivation and rejection.[111] Thus, there is a great deal of evidence for early developmental trauma causing a person to lose their empathy in this uniquely borderline way (though this is not a necessary cause). Again, it brings us back to a more sympathetic view of borderlines, as those who have suffered trauma. And it highlights the more general point that one effect of trauma can be a reduction in empathy.

The borderline brain

Remarkably, despite the unstable behaviour of Type Bs, scientists have managed to study their brains, which are definitely different in much of the empathy circuit.

First, there is decreased binding of neurotransmitters to one of the serotonin[xxiv] receptors.[112] Just as we might expect, these abnormalities occur in brain regions within the empathy circuit: the ventromedial prefrontal cortex (vMPFC) and middle cingulate cortex (MCC), and areas of the temporal lobe, among other areas.[112, 113] Neuroimaging also reveals abnormalities in the empathy circuit in the Type B brain, particularly under-activity in the orbital frontal cortex (OFC)/vMPFC, and in the temporal cortex, all parts of the empathy circuit. And when reading a script about 'abandonment', there is less activity in empathy brain regions such as the amygdala, the vMPFC and MCC, the inferior frontal gyrus (IFG) and the superior temporal sulcus (STS). Other studies have found increased amygdala activity on both sides of the brain during emotionally aversive slides. Similarly, while looking at emotional faces, borderlines show increased left amygdala activity.[114–121] Finally, a recent study found that when Type B individuals play a 'trust' game, they show no signs of being able to maintain or repair broken attempts to co-operate with other individuals. Neural markers related to co-operative and trusting gestures (the anterior insula or AI), active in typical individuals, were completely absent in Type B individuals.[122]

A novel approach has been to follow up people who were abused as children and scan their brains. It is novel because it is prospective rather than retrospective: the emotional damage was done in childhood and the scientific question is 'what happens to their brain?' Not all of them will be Type Bs, but a significant proportion will be. Such people again have abnormalities in the empathy circuit, such as having a smaller amygdala. This is also true of women who were sexually abused, who later show less grey matter in their left medial temporal cortex, compared to non-abused women. Smaller hippocampal volume is also found in people who experienced a trauma and went on to develop post-traumatic stress disorder (PTSD).[123-129] One interpretation of all this evidence is that the early negative experiences of abuse and neglect change how the brain turns out. But the key point is that the zero degrees of empathy in borderlines arises from abnormalities in the empathy circuit of the brain.

My aim in describing borderlines as one form of zero degrees of empathy is not to add to their already considerable level of suffering, by using a term that could be stigmatizing. Stigmatizing someone is never acceptable. But it is to draw attention to what happens to their empathy circuit when they are having a crisis, and how they lose sight of the other person as someone with feelings. And this new view has direct treatment implications: help the person with their empathy. This approach, (called 'mentalization-based therapy' or MBT, developed at University College London by clinicians Peter Fonagy and Anthony Bateman) is already showing potential benefits.

ZERO-NEGATIVE TYPE P

Our next encounter with a form of zero degrees of empathy is the psychopath (or Type P). When we meet the psychopath we see a person who shares that same total preoccupation with oneself as we saw in Type B. But, in this case, there is a willingness to do *whatever it takes* to satisfy their desires. This might take the form of a hair-trigger violent reaction to the smallest thing that thwarts them. Or it might take the form of cold, calculated cruelty. Sometimes the mindless aggression is not triggered by a perceived threat but by the need to dominate, to get what one wants, a complete detachment from another person's feelings, and possibly even some pleasure at seeing someone else suffer. (The Germans have a word for this: *schadenfreude*.[xxv])

I think you'll find it a small step to conceptualize Type P as what some people call 'evil', but the questions we keep returning to in this book are whether this is the result of zero degrees of empathy, and if this is in turn the result of the empathy circuit not developing and functioning in the normal way. But first let's look at a real case of a psychopath.

Paul: Type P

Paul (not his real name, to protect his identity) is twenty-eight years old and is currently detained in a secure prison after being found guilty of murder. I was asked to conduct a diagnostic interview with him by his lawyer, and, because his violence meant it could have been unsafe for him to come to our clinic, I went to see him in the prison. He told me how he had wound up in jail. He insisted he wasn't guilty because the man he stabbed had provoked him by looking at him from across the bar. Paul had gone over to the man and said, 'Why were you staring at me?' The man had replied, I assume truthfully: 'I wasn't staring at you. I was simply looking around the bar.' Paul had felt incensed by the man's answer, believing it to be disrespectful, and felt he needed to be taught a lesson. He picked up a beer bottle, smashed it on the table, and plunged the jagged end deep into the man's face.

Like me, the barrister at Paul's trial was shocked by the apparent lack of remorse and the self-righteousness of his plea of not guilty. In my questioning I probed further for some evidence of moral conscience. Paul was adamant that he had simply defended himself.

'He humiliated me in public. I had to show him I wasn't a doormat.'

I asked, 'Do you believe you did anything wrong?'

Paul replied, 'People have treated me like shit all my life. I'm not taking it from no one no more. If someone shows me disrespect, they deserve what they get.'

I probed further: 'Are you sorry that he died?' I waited to hear Paul's answer, holding my breath. He replied with anger in his voice:

'Were the kids at school sorry when they bullied me? Was my boss sorry when he fired me? Was my neighbour sorry when he deliberately hit my car? And you ask me if I'm sorry that that piece of shit died? Of course I'm not sorry. He had it coming to him. No one's ever been sorry for how they've treated me. Why should I give a fuck about him?'

This wasn't Paul's first offence. He had been in prison six times since he left school at sixteen, for offences that include shoplifting, drug dealing, rape and violent assault. He'd left school with no qualifications, and his career of criminal behaviour had begun when he was as young as thirteen, when he had set fire to the school gym and sat in a tree across a field to watch it burn. He was expelled and from there went to three more schools, each time being expelled for aggression – starting fights in the playground, attacking a teacher who asked him to be quiet, and even jumping on someone's head when they wouldn't let him join the football team.

As a very young child, the warning signs had been there. At eight years old, he was cruel to his cat, finding it amusing to tie a brick to her back leg and to film her trying to walk. For as long as his mother could remember, Paul had told lies, about both small things (saying he had done his homework when he hadn't) and bigger things (saying he had gone to school when he hadn't). Truanting led to staying out all night, even at twelve years old, without telling his parents or getting their permission.

Stepping back from Paul

Paul is clearly not the kind of guy you want to live anywhere near. Many would not hesitate to describe him as 'evil'. He is a psychopath – though to give him the proper diagnostic label, we should say he has Anti-Social Personality Disorder (see Appendix 2 for the list of 'symptoms' required for this diagnosis). He earns this label because he shows 'a pervasive pattern of disregard for and violation of the rights of others that begins in childhood or adolescence, and continues into adulthood'.[131] Anti-Social Personality Disorder is diagnosed if someone is over eighteen years old and if they previously had a different diagnosis, Conduct Disorder, in childhood. In Paul's case, he clearly did. Not all cases of Conduct Disorder grow up into Anti-Social Personality Disorder, but many do (at least 40 per cent).

In the general population, about 3 per cent of males (but only 1 per cent of females) have Anti-Social Personality Disorder. In prison samples, the rates are – perhaps unsurprisingly – much higher: about half of all male inmates would warrant this diagnosis, and a quarter of all female inmates.[132] And some people with Anti-Social Personality Disorder – like Paul – are psychopaths.

Psychopaths

The full name for Paul's condition is Psychopathic Personality Disorder – or what I call Zero-Negative Type P. About 15 per cent of prison samples are psychopaths, and just less than 1 per cent of males in the general population.[133] The concept of the psychopath goes back to 1941, to Hervey Cleckley's[xxvi] book *The Mask of Sanity*.[134] As its title suggests, Cleckley was concerned with how to recognize a psychopath if he or she is convincingly pretending to be normal. He argued that psychopaths show:

- superficial charm
- a lack of anxiety or guilt
- undependability and dishonesty
- egocentricity
- an inability to form lasting intimate relationships
- a failure to learn from punishment
- poverty of emotions
- a lack of insight into the impact of their behaviour, and
- a failure to plan ahead.

Let's look at the second of these a little more closely: *a lack of anxiety or guilt*. To me, these two emotions are connected to Type Ps very differently. Clearly, someone who lacks guilt will be capable of doing bad things without worrying about how they themselves will feel later, let alone worrying how someone else might feel. If you have empathy you will be capable of feeling guilt, while if you lack empathy, you won't. This might make you think that guilt and empathy is one and the same thing: clearly this cannot be true, since a person can feel guilt (e.g., that they went through a red traffic light) without necessarily feeling empathy. So empathy can give rise to guilt but guilt is not proof of empathy. The relationship between anxiety and psychopathic behaviour is also important, since someone who lacks anxiety will be capable of doing bad things without worrying about being punished. But anxiety by itself is not part of empathy. It merely provides a rationale for why one might not hurt another person.

Notice that several of the features in the above list also centre on a lack of empathy: a *lack of insight* into the impact of his or her behaviour, and *egocentricity*. As we discussed in Chapter 2, intrinsic to poor empathy is lack of self-awareness, which is probably synonymous with a lack of insight. Psychiatrists are very fond of the term 'insight', and here we see the considerable overlap between these concepts. Take for example a person who hurts someone without meaning to (perhaps by saying the wrong thing). Here, the lack of insight is part and parcel of the lack of empathy. In terms of how willing we are to forgive an unempathic act, one might judge that if we hurt another person without realizing it, this is less bad than if we hurt someone else knowingly. Hurting someone knowingly is sometimes also referred to as 'premeditated'. From Cleckley's definition, a psychopath might be capable of both kinds of unempathic act. Lacking any sense of guilt might mean one could hurt a person knowing they would indeed hurt; but lacking any insight into the impact of one's behaviour means that one might hurt someone without realizing it.

Interestingly, Cleckley's definition of a psychopath makes no mention of physical aggression or of breaking the law, which hints at how psychopaths may not come to the attention of the criminal justice system and may be at large in society. They may be the 'snakes in suits' in any workplace.[135] While this phrase has become somewhat clichéd, I know of no better way to convey the idea of how Type P might be camouflaged. Clearly, some psychopaths hurt others through physical aggression, but the breakthrough in Cleckley's formulation was to extend this concept to those who are aggressive in more subtle, invisible ways. A milder form of Type P might be what is sometimes called the 'Machiavellian' personality type, or people who are what Richard Christie and Florence Geis called 'high Machs': individuals who use others for their own self-promotion. They will lie to get what they want.[136]

We saw that a major risk factor in becoming Type B is one's experience of parental rejection in childhood. I want to dwell on this a bit longer, because how your mother (or father) treated you turns out to be very important both for the development of healthy empathy, and for the risk of becoming Zero-Negative Type P as well. Parental rejection can lead to a child growing up to become violent or a psychopath. It may not be the only factor, but it can be an important one. One reason why parental rejection might be linked to a child developing aggression in adulthood is that inside – emotionally – the child is quietly *raging* against the parental rejection and is developing high levels of hate. Such extreme, negative emotions are hard to regulate. The child has to vent their rage somewhere and, if as a child they were unable to express it towards the rejecting parent, it may build up, like steam in a pressure cooker, just waiting to be vented in adolescence and adulthood. The result can be explosive violence.

Parental rejection was famously studied by John Bowlby, a psychoanalyst and child psychiatrist at the Tavistock Clinic in London. It was here that he developed his remarkable Attachment Theory that explored (on the negative side) the consequences of parental rejection and (on the positive side) the consequences of parental affection. I say remarkable because the theory made predictions that have been amply proven and are socially extremely important.

According to Bowlby, the infant uses the caregiver as a 'secure base' from which to explore the world, feeling that, when they move away from their parent, they can also return to him or her for 'emotional refuelling'. (The caregiver is often but not necessarily the child's biological mother or father.) By giving praise, reassurance and a feeling of safety, the caregiver's affection helps the child manage his or her anxiety, develop self-confidence, and trust in the security of the relationship.

My paraphrase of Bowlby's theory is this: what the caregiver gives his or her child in those first few critical years is like an *internal pot of gold*. The idea – which builds on Freud's insight – is that what a parent can give his or her child by way of filling the child up with positive emotions is a gift more precious than anything material. That internal pot of gold is something the child can carry inside throughout their life, even if they become a penniless refugee or are beset by other challenges. This internal pot of gold is what gives the individual the strength to deal with challenges, the ability to bounce back from setbacks, and the ability to show affection and enjoy intimacy with others, in other relationships. It overlaps with what London child psychiatrist Michael Rutter refers to as 'resilience'.[137]

Bringing this back to psychopaths (and other forms of Anti-Social Personality Disorder), if you trace backwards, such individuals typically have a higher rate of what Bowlby called 'insecure attachment'.[xxvii] [138, 139] Bowlby's original study, aptly published in 1944, was a careful look at adolescent delinquency, and was entitled *Forty-Four Juvenile Thieves, Their Characters and Home Lives*. It was the impetus for his theory. What I find important in this work is that it argues that security of early attachment between an infant and his or her caregiver predicts not just how emotionally well-adjusted an individual turns out as an adult, but also predicts their *moral* development. (Moral development and empathy are not one and the same thing, since it is possible to develop a strong moral code even in the absence of empathy. We'll come back to this later.)

Bowlby's forty-four thieves were – in his chilling words – 'affectionless psychopaths'. They showed shallow relationships, having been in and out of children's homes or institutions, forming superficial relationships with dozens – if not hundreds – of adults. In Bowlby's view, deep, trusting relationships with just one or a small number of caregivers are vital. Such secure relationships promote both social development (popularity at school, good social skills, turn-taking, sharing) and language development (better communication). Even more, securely attached infants later also develop better empathy and 'theory of mind' (being able to accurately infer others' thoughts). Those with insecure attachments have a higher rate of social difficulties, including anti-social behaviour, and, later in life, a higher risk of divorce in adulthood.

Bowlby studied psychology as part of medicine at my college (Trinity College) in Cambridge. He later forged close links with Cambridge ethologist Robert Hinde, who extended Harry Harlow's seminal studies of monkeys reared without mothers to see the effects of maternal deprivation. This animal model – while ethically questionable[xxviii] – has taught us a lot about how, in social primates (whether humans or monkeys), a difficult attachment relationship not only increases the risk of the monkey developing aggression, mistakenly interpreting friendly approaches as aggressive, but also in turn increases the risk of the child growing up to become a parent who is harsh and abusive.[140]

Now you can see why I describe Bowlby's Attachment Theory as remarkable. It predicts trans-generational effects. Astonishingly, it also predicts effects outside the narrow realm of social development, in that securely attached infants grow up to become academically more successful at school. This may be because the 'internal pot of gold' gives the child that sense of self-confidence and self-esteem to have the courage to explore new areas of learning, and to persist in the face of failure. It may also be that secure attachment makes the child a better mind-reader, both of someone else's and of their own mind, so that they can reflect on what they know and don't know, and therefore can learn how to learn. Following his important study of the forty-four thieves, Bowlby was commissioned by the World Health Organization in 1951 to write a report, *Maternal Care and Mental Health*, which transformed how we care for young children in both schools and hospitals, making such environments more child-friendly and parent-friendly.[xxix] What other psychological theory has had such far-reaching impact?[141]

Clearly insecure attachment is on a spectrum, and relevant to the development of a psychopath are the negative experiences at the most severe end that may go along with childhood separation, such as inconsistent parental discipline, parental alcoholism, lack of supervision, physical, sexual or emotional abuse, or complete abandonment.[142] The argument – from the 'internal pot of gold' – is that insecure attachment of this more extreme form increases your risk of becoming Zero-Negative.[143]

My old friend Peter Fonagy is a professor of psychoanalysis at University College London and Director of the Anna Freud Centre in Hampstead in London. He is one of those rare scientists who has taken interesting ideas from psychoanalysis and tried to test them empirically. He argues that during the attachment relationship, the infant tries to 'mentalize' their caregiver's mind. The child's relationship with his or her parents is the crucible for learning about other people. The child not only imagines what their mother is thinking or feeling about people and things in the immediate environment, but, more importantly, what their mother is thinking or feeling about *them*. He argues that developing empathy proceeds well only if it is safe to imagine another person's thoughts and feelings.

But if when you mentalize you imagine that your mother hates you or wishes you didn't exist, this could derail the development of empathy. It is certainly an interesting argument, and there is some evidence that fits the idea that parental behaviour contributes to a child's empathy. For example, parents who discipline their child by discussing the consequences of their actions produce children who have better moral development, compared to children whose parents use authoritarian methods and punishment.[144] And parents who use empathy to socialize their children also produce children who are less likely to commit offences, compared to the children of parents who use physical punishment.

The Psychopathic Mind

Moving from the early family environment, we can go a little deeper to probe what is going on within the mind of a psychopath. It will come as no surprise that, on questionnaire measures of empathy, psychopaths score lower than others. This can be seen, for example, on the Interpersonal Reactivity Index (IRI).[145] However, self-report is notoriously unreliable with psychopaths, since they typically lie to hide their true nature. To avoid this, researchers have resorted to physiological measures of autonomic arousal – how stirred up you become when you hear or see emotional material.[146, 147] Typically what is measured is galvanic skin response (GSR) – how much you sweat on the palms of your hands when shown emotionally charged material. This reveals that psychopaths have reduced autonomic responsiveness (they are less aroused) while looking at pictures of individuals in distress. This implies they have reduced 'affective' empathy.

Psychopaths are also worse at naming fearful emotional expressions.[148,149] However, the fact that people who are Type P often deceive others suggests that their 'cognitive empathy' is frequently intact. A clue that psychopaths are not processing emotional material in the normal way is that, whereas most people are faster to judge 'is this a word?' when they are shown emotional words (relative to their speed at judging neutral words), psychopaths do not show a difference between emotional and neutral words. A method to measure how aroused you are by emotional material is to use event-related potentials (ERP). These show electrical activity in the brain measured by placing electrodes on your scalp. Psychopaths do not show the usual increase in brain activity over the central and parietal regions of the brain in response to emotional words.[150, 151] As we saw with Paul, one other difference in those who are aggressive is the tendency to interpret ambiguous situations as if the other person has hostile intent. This has been found in children with conduct disorder, some of whom go on to become psychopaths, and is referred to as an 'attributional bias',[152] a clear example of the cognitive aspect of empathy not working accurately.

One view of the psychopathic mind is that they are simply *amoral*. The classic test of morality was developed by Kohlberg: you are asked to read a story and judge the morality of the story's character. The famous example is of the husband who breaks into the chemist shop to steal an anti-cancer drug for his wife, who is dying of cancer, because the chemist refuses to sell the drug for less than $2000 (even though it cost the chemist only $200 to make). You are asked to judge if the husband was wrong or not. The more complex your ability to reason about such moral dilemmas, the more advanced your moral reasoning is judged to be. If you can see two sides of an argument, or that context might change the rights and wrongs of an act, this is taken as a sign that you have a subtler mind than someone who simply reasons on the basis of rules. Contrary to what one might expect, psychopaths do not necessarily score lower on such tests.[153] This may be because psychopaths can say one thing, even though in their day-to-day life they will do another.

Kohlberg's method of measuring moral reasoning is not the only approach. On Elliot Turiel's tests of moral reasoning, the stories describe not just moral transgressions – acts that violate human rights (e.g., hurting another person) – but also conventional transgressions – acts that violate social conventions (e.g., talking in a library). You are asked to judge how bad an action was, and whether it would still be wrong if there was no rule banning it. By four years old most children can tell the difference between these two types of transgressions, and recognize that while you can change the rules for conventional trans-

I hope you feel Better
mommy
love
Isabella
x x x x
(and matthew)

my detailes

B

B~

909788809-5

gressions so that the act is no longer a transgression (you can announce that in *this* particular library, talking *is* allowed), if you modify the rule for a moral transgression (announcing it is now legal to hurt others) that doesn't make the act any less bad than before.[154] Psychopaths have trouble with this kind of distinction, as do children with anti-social behaviour.[148, 155]

So this tells us that, as well as not showing emotional reactions to others' distress in the normal way, psychopaths are also blunted in their moral development. But is this simply because psychopaths are less intelligent? There is a clear link between low IQ, low socio-economic status (SES), and anti-social behaviour. The link between low IQ and low SES could be because in poorer neighbourhoods there is a greater likelihood of poorer education. But why should low IQ and low SES increase your risk of developing anti-social behaviour? One reason could be because, without educational qualifications or a job, crime may be a way to make a living. Low IQ may also make it harder for someone to imagine the consequences of getting caught. But the fact that intelligent psychopaths exist shows that low intelligence cannot explain everyone who becomes a psychopath, and the fact that empathic individuals with low IQ also exist, proves that empathy and IQ must be independent.

Jeffrey Gray was a professor of psychology in London's Institute of Psychiatry whom I had the pleasure of working with in the early 1990s. He developed a model of anxiety he called the Behavioural Inhibition System (BIS), located in the septo-hippocampal brain network, the system that allows an animal to learn the emotional consequences (reward or punishment) of its actions. It was a bold model when he put it forward in 1982[156] and it inspired Joseph Newman at the University of Wisconsin-Madison to argue that psychopaths had an *under-active* BIS, while anxious people had an overactive BIS.[xxx] Newman's interesting idea is that psychopaths basically have a problem in thinking about the consequences of their actions, since damage to the BIS leads an animal to repeat behaviours that elicit punishment.

Newman argues this is the core problem in psychopaths – they do not learn to *fear punishment*. No wonder they do things that they know might get them into trouble. He argues this explains why psychopaths make errors on tasks where you have to learn which (otherwise neutral) numbers are rewarding and which ones are not,[157] and why they fail to change their behaviour even when an action is no longer rewarding and is leading to punishment. For example, given a deck of cards to play with, where each card leads to winning a reward, children with psychopathic traits continue playing even when the cards no longer lead to rewards.[158] Nowadays we recognize that there are many 'fear pathways' in the brain, and that the amygdala also plays a key role in the experience of fear. A problem for Joseph Newman's account is that it emphasizes the importance of anxiety in how children are socialized, but many children are socialized not just through fear of punishment but through discussion about how the other person feels (empathy).[159]

Nevertheless, the idea that *psychopaths lack fear* was an important insight. In *The Mask of Sanity*, Hervey Cleckley wrote, 'Within himself he appears almost as incapable of anxiety as of profound remorse.'[160] This appears to be true of the so-called 'callous sub-group',[161] and behavioural geneticist David Lykken at the University of Minnesota tested this by using a 'conditioning' experiment: an electric shock paired with the sound of a buzzer. 'Normal' individuals developed 'electrodermal fear' (sweating) when hearing the buzzer (that is, the buzzer had become a 'conditioned stimulus'). In contrast, psychopaths showed less electrodermal fear to the buzzer – they did not acquire the 'conditioned response' to the threat. They also show less of a startle reflex (an automatic jump) to a loud sound, or to an object looming towards them.[147, 162–164] All this suggests a very specific kind of learning difficulty involving lower fear of punishment.

Clearly Type Ps differ in important ways to Type Bs, but they share the core feature of being Zero-Negative. This core represents a shared endpoint in development. Crucially, their zero degrees of empathy can result in them doing cruel things to others. When we come to look at their brain, we should expect to see the same underlying empathy circuitry to be affected.

The Psychopathic Brain

Scientists have managed to persuade psychopaths to climb into the fMRI scanner, to enable us to understand the neural basis of empathy and of its absence. Just as one might predict, abnormalities in the empathy circuit are seen: aggressive people show less ventromedial prefrontal cortex (vMPFC) activity,[165] and the higher a person scores on the Psychopathy Checklist-Revised (PCL-R),[xxxi] the less activity they showed in the orbitofrontal cortex(OFC)/ vMPFC and temporal regions.[166] These are squarely in the empathy circuit. Furthermore, when scientists map out the connections between the vMPFC/OFC and amygdala, they find the integrity of this tract is reduced in psychopaths and this predicts scores on the Psychopathy Checklist.[167] Males on average are also much more prone to anti-social behaviour. This sex difference is predominantly explained by sex differences in the size of the OFC. Males have a smaller OFC volume compared to females, and males who exhibited increasing anti-social behaviour have even smaller OFC.[168]

One view of the psychopathic brain is that the primary problem is located in the frontal lobes, since these are meant to provide 'executive' control over action, stopping us from doing what could lead to punishment. Neuroanatomically, this is too simplistic for several reasons. First, the frontal lobe takes up at least a third of the brain, so as an explanation it is way too broad. Second, the frontal lobe can be segmented, and patients with damage in the OFC/vMPFC (but not in the dorsolateral segment) have increased levels of aggression. This shows the abnormality is occurring within the empathy circuitry within the frontal lobes, not the whole of the frontal lobes. Recall that patients with damage in the vMPFC show reduced heart rate arousal to emotionally distressing stimuli and also continue to gamble on tasks even when they are no longer winning (or being rewarded).[169,170] Recall that Phineas Gage suffered damage to his entire OFC and vMPFC, and began showing signs of callous, rude, irreverent and disinhibited behaviour. All of these are signals of difficulties in using emotions like embarrassment and guilt to regulate one's own social behavior.[29, 30, 171] Patients with damage to the OFC/vMPFC show changes in their moral judgements. For example, they would judge it morally acceptable to be personally involved in killing one person in order to save the lives of five others (a judgement that most people would deem to be unacceptable).[172] It turns out that such patients judge moral decisions in this way because they pay less attention to their own or others' *intentions*. Thus, vMPFC-lesion patients judged *attempted* acts to harm another person as more morally permissible than did a control group.[173] In this way, as we saw earlier, patients with damage to this specific area of the prefrontal cortex resemble psychopaths.

For this reason, Damasio's vMPFC somatic marker theory (which we encountered in Chapter 2) could explain Type P. This has a lot of plausibility, though it is surrounded by debate since individuals without 'autonomic' arousal nevertheless perform normally on a classic gambling task.[174, 175] It may be that abnormalities in the vMPFC/OFC lead to aggressive anti-social behaviour, but it may not necessarily be because these individuals have problems reading their own 'somatic' states. Another problem is that, while damage to the vMPFC can cause 'reactive' aggression (the hair-trigger anger reaction), it typically does not cause 'instrumental' aggression (the cold, calculated, premeditated type of cruelty). So, as a model of the Type P brain, it misses out a key aspect of their behaviour, since psychopaths can show an increase in both. Thirdly, patients with lesions in the vMPFC also show less autonomic arousal to other emotional stimuli (like images of nudity), whereas psychopaths tend to only show this reduction to threatening or distressing stimuli. This suggests the very particular form of zero degrees of empathy seen in psychopaths is not only simply a problem with the vMPFC.

Adrian Raine and his colleagues have looked at the brains of murderers (those 'pleading not guilty by reason of insanity'). They again found differences in the empathy circuit, in the vMPFC, the amygdala and superior temporal lobe (STS).[176, 177] Reduced activity in the orbitofrontal cortex was also found in aggressive people in a novel study comparing people with different personality disorders.[178]

The evidence of the empathy circuit being involved in aggression gets additional support from a remarkable study by neuroscientist Jean Decety and colleagues in the University of Chicago, of teenagers with Conduct Disorder who had all been involved in physical fights. As we mentioned earlier, a proportion of these kids grow up to be Type P. In this study the teenagers either watched films where someone got hurt accidentally (e.g., something just happened to drop on their hand) or where someone got hurt deliberately (e.g., someone's hand got stepped on). The aggressive teenagers showed more activity in both the amygdala and in the reward circuit (the ventral striatum) during the films showing deliberate infliction of pain on another person. Hypersensitivity of the reward circuitry[179] may be of key importance in anti-social behaviour/Type P.

The implication is that they actually *enjoy* seeing another person suffer. That German word *schadenfreude* (experiencing pleasure at someone else's pain) which we mentioned earlier comes to mind. The other difference in this study was that the aggressive teenagers did not show activity in parts of the empathy circuit like the temporoparietal junction (TPJ), an area of the brain normally used in understanding intentions when making moral judgements,[180-182] or in the anterior insula (AI) and middle cingulate cortex (MCC) (recall that these are part of the 'pain matrix'). And in Washington, working at the National Institutes of Health (NIH), James Blair has argued persuasively that in the psychopath the amygdala is not working normally. This claim is well supported by a neuroimaging study showing less amygdala activity in psychopaths while they are experiencing aversive conditioning.[183] So, we can say that the Type P brain shows lots of evidence of abnormalities in the empathy circuitry.

The effects of early stress on the empathy circuit

It begs the question as to how all these changes to the brain have come about. Given the role of the environment, especially the association with neglect and abuse in childhood, there is evidence that early stress affects how well the hippocampus functions,[184] and how active the neural systems are that respond to threat. Stress can also affect your hormonal response to threat. Prolonged exposure to stress isn't good for your brain. The amygdala is one of the brain regions that respond to stress or threat.[185] When it does, it triggers the hypothalamus to trigger the pituitary gland to release a hormone called ACTH (adrenocorticotropic hormone). This is then carried by the blood from the brain down to the adrenal gland where it triggers the release of another hormone, cortisol.

Cortisol is often called the 'stress hormone' because it is a good indicator of when an animal is under stress. There are receptors for cortisol in the hippocampus that allow the animal to regulate the stress response. Remarkably, too much stress can damage and shrink your hippocampus, irreversibly.[186, 187] Stress can also cause 'aborization' of one part of the amygdala,[xxxii] in which nerve cells start branching more than normal, becoming over-reactive.[188]

This is very relevant to what earlier we called 'reactive aggression', seen in both humans and other animals. It is part of the 'fight or flight' self-defence system. A small threat usually leads an animal to freeze, to avoid getting any closer to the threat and enabling the animal to take stock of what to do next. Freezing can also minimize the risk of being attacked if the aggressor is responsive to your movement or is looking for a sign that you are submissive. If the threat gets a bit closer this typically leads to 'escape' behaviour. A bigger and closer threat, where escape is not an option, typically leads an animal to show reactive aggression.

The signal to show reactive aggression comes both from the amygdala (since this region in the empathy circuit is highly active during the experience of fear) and from areas of the frontal cortex, which can either put the brakes on, to enable self-regulation and inhibition, or release the brakes to launch an attack against the perceived threat. So reactive aggression could be over-reactive because your amygdala is overactive (e.g., during periods of depression and anxiety,[189] or due to the prolonged exposure to early stress, or for genetic reasons[190]) and/ or if your prefrontal cortex is under-active (such that you cannot inhibit your reactive aggression).[191] Once again, we see that abnormalities in key regions in the empathy circuit can produce reduced or even zero degrees of empathy.

NIH cognitive neuroscientist James Blair has put forward an alternative model of what causes a person to become Type P. He worked at the Medical Research Council's Cognitive Development Unit in London where I also did my early research. During his PhD work the young James Blair enthusiastically went to meet psychopaths who were locked up in maximum-security facilities such as Broadmoor Hospital. He developed a model that he called the Violence Inhibition Mechanism (VIM). Sounds relevant? He argued that when we (and this is true in many other animals too) see the distress of a conspecific (a member of the same species), we have an automatic reaction to reduce the other person/animal's distress.

Blair sees the VIM as a system that is automatically activated whenever you see sad or distressed facial expressions in others, or hear these emotions in their voice. It tells you 'someone is upset' and it leads to increased autonomic arousal (your heart starts beating faster, you start sweating more) and activation of the threat system in the brain, causing you to freeze. In other words, in the face of someone else's distress, you inhibit what you are doing. Presumably this is highly adaptive in preventing one animal from inflicting violence on another. All they have to do is cry out or wince in pain for you to stop whatever you were doing, and this would include any actions of yours that might be causing their pain. According to Blair, psychopaths have an under-active VIM.

Some evidence to support this is that psychopaths have reduced autonomic arousal to the distress of others.[146] However, the VIM model can't easily account for the results showing that psychopaths continue to play card gambling games even when they are no longer rewarding – since in these games there are presumably no distress cues. Nor can his model readily explain why affectionate parenting (of the kind Bowlby argued promoted secure attachment) also leads to better socialization, since in the lives of such children there are presumably few if any cues of distress.

So, there is more than ample evidence that in Type P there are abnormalities in the empathy circuit of the brain. This is one more piece of evidence for the argument that instead of using the term 'evil' we should talk about reduced (or even absent) empathy. But there is just one more Zero-Negative type we have yet to meet, if you're still willing to pursue this journey with me: Type N (or the narcissist).

JAMES: ZERO-NEGATIVE TYPE N

James is sixty-four years old. Like Carol, James came to our diagnostic clinic. He feels angry at the world. He feels he has only done good things all his life, and that others have not reciprocated. As a result, he feels he has been badly treated by society.

'I have tried to live a good life, always helping others, supporting my family, visiting sick friends and relatives in hospital, helping others. And guess what? Other people are shits. They don't bother helping me. They don't visit, they don't call, they even cross the road when they see me coming. I eat alone everyday. You wouldn't treat a dog the way people treat me. I'm entitled to friendship just like everyone else, so why do they offer it to others and not to me?'

The key word here is 'entitled'. James feels he has an automatic right to be treated well, irrespective of how he treats others. When you talk to James it becomes apparent after a few minutes that all he talks about is himself and his family, his needs and desires. If you believed his account, his children are more talented than anyone else's, he is superior to other people, he is more attractive than anyone else, and in his mind his social status is above others. It's as if nothing or no one of any importance exists outside himself and his children. He is oblivious to how other people listening to him might feel. It is as if they are there to be his audience, listening to how great he is, and their role is to agree with him and admire him. When people murmur politely he takes this as confirmation of his own specialness, and he is elated for a while. But soon his mood plummets, and he reverts to sounding depressed, negative and complaining. If you ask James why he is so negative he says:

'People should treat me better. Since my wife died I live alone. No one bothers to cook for me, phone me, or even knock on my door. It's as if I'm some kind of social leper. Anyone would think I had some kind of disease.'

When James goes to a restaurant, he demands the best table. He assumes he can go straight to the front of the queue, and he becomes abusive to the waiter when his food does not arrive quickly. If he goes to hospital, he harasses the receptionist, demanding to be seen before other patients. 'If I don't see the doctor immediately I'm putting in a complaint!' When he phones up for an engineer to fix an appliance at home, he demands they come immediately. He constantly complains his children are bad because they don't phone him or visit him enough. When they do, he verbally abuses them, telling them they are selfish for not giving him any attention. They know that, however much attention they give him, his needs are so great that whatever they do is never enough. When he feels important, for example when he flies business class, he temporarily feels elated. When he feels people aren't giving him enough attention, if for example he is seated at the end of a table during a family gathering, he feels badly treated, and will look angry and be critical. He has no idea that his behaviour only drives others further away, and when they avoid him he takes this as confirmation that they are bad people, that the problem is with them rather than him.

If he meets people who are in a position of influence and could be of some help to him, he turns on his charm and is fun and humorous, storing up information on how they might be of value to him in the future. But, if someone cannot give him anything that he needs, they suddenly become unimportant. 'They are of no value to me,' he will say. He is unaware how this reflects his pattern of using people shamelessly, taking as much as he can from them, discarding them when they are of no use to him. When he goes to the local church community centre and people ask him how he is, he vents his criticisms: nothing works properly, people have let him down, services are under par. His diatribe is so negative that it leaves some people wanting to walk away. He has no idea what others might find rude and he often makes offensive remarks. In answer to the question 'How are you?' he often replies sarcastically: 'Thanks for the invitation to dinner', leaving the questioner in an awkward silence. If people ask James what he has been doing he usually mentions he is writing his autobiography, which he alone thinks is interesting. If women show an interest in him, he is instantly flirtatious. As soon as they turn their attention away, or express an alternative view to his, he denigrates and criticizes them.

Stepping back from James

The narcissist (Type N) is recognizably different from the psychopath (Type P) and the borderline (Type B) we met earlier. In one way, their zero degrees of empathy renders them deeply self-centred, but while they may say and do things that offend others, they may not commit cruel acts. Rather, narcissists think they are much better than other people, as if they have special gifts that others lack, in the absence of any humility. Indeed, the continuous boastfulness and self-promotion is partly what others find offensive, not because of jealousy but as indicators of the narcissist's total self-preoccupation. The narcissist, like the other Zero-Negative forms, fails to recognize the importance of relationships being two-way. For those who have zero degrees of empathy, relationships are not really relationships because they are one way. This is even evident in how much the narcissist talks. There is no attempt to make space in the conversation for the other person, or to find out about the other person. The narcissist simply lectures, holding forth about him or herself, and they decide when to end the conversation. They have monologues, not dialogues.

Some psychodynamic thinkers would regard a modicum of narcissism as both necessary, normative and healthy, the opposite being someone who does not like themselves.[192, 193] This implies narcissism itself lies on a spectrum of traits, and becomes 'pathological' only in the extreme case of someone who *only* cares about him or herself and cares about others only if they are useful to him or her. Expressed differently, other people are exploited for their usefulness to the narcissist. In that sense, they are being used as objects (in the jargon, as 'self-objects').

Narcissism can take different forms in different people. (See Appendix 2 for the list of their 'diagnostic symptoms'.) Some are very outgoing, wanting to steal the limelight, being the boss of a company or the leader of a group. Others appear socially withdrawn as if shy, but they still have the sense of entitlement, angry that others are not doing more for them, and expecting others to run to them, rather than expecting to meet others half way. Yet others may become dangerous, and this personality type has sometimes been thought to underlie the serial killer.[194] Narcissists are about 1 per cent of the general population, though much more common (making up to 16 per cent) in those attending clinics for mental health issues. Unlike Type B, at least half to three-quarters are male. Like Types P or B, early emotional abuse has been suggested as a possible cause of Type N, again reminding us of the importance of that internal pot of gold. But unlike the other Zero-Negative types, it is speculated that excessive admiration, excessive praise for their good looks or talents, over-indulgence, and being over-valued in the absence of realistic feedback (by parents) may also contribute to why someone ends up as Type N. By comparison to Types P or B, there is very little research into Type N, a gap that needs to be filled. My own view is that, of these three forms of Zero-Negative personalities, Type N may be no less easy for others but may be less likely to lead to acts of cruelty. This is precisely the kind of question we need more information about though.

Psychiatry groups these three ways of becoming Zero-Negative under the heading of 'personality disorders', which of course they all are. But for me the blindingly obvious characteristic they all share is they are all at zero degrees of empathy. In the case of Type B, this may fluctuate depending on the individual's capacity for self-control of their emotional state, such that in between crises their empathy may recover, before it crashes again. My prediction was that they should all show abnormalities in the empathy circuitry in the brain. What we have seen is that, whether someone loses their empathy by becoming Type B or Type P, the *same* neural circuitry is affected. We can predict similar abnormalities in the empathy circuit in Type N will be found, though these studies have yet to be done. All this is building a more complete picture of empathy and how someone becomes Zero-Negative.

This of course raises the question as to why one individual is Type P and another is Type B or Type N. Here we must assume the routes to the common endpoint are different, either in terms of different genes or different environmental factors, or both. We will return to this in Chapter 5. In this sense, the functioning of the empathy circuit is the final common pathway that determines if a person is in a state where they could hurt another person.

The distinction between transient or permanent under-activity of the empathy circuit echoes the distinction in personality psychology of 'states' vs. 'traits'. 'States' are fluctuations in a psychological or neural system, induced by a particular context, and are reversible. We all know the kinds of short-term states we can enter which can compromise our empathy. These include being drunk, tired, impatient, or stressed, where we might say or do the wrong thing to someone else, and later regret it. The feeling of regret is a sign of our empathy circuit coming back on, but the fact that we say or do the wrong thing is nevertheless – at that moment – a fluctuation in our empathy circuit.

In contrast, 'traits' are permanent, crystallized configurations of a psychological or neural system, enduring across different contexts, and are irreversible.

In personality psychology, clusters of traits constitute personality types (such as introverts or extraverts), and Types B, P and N are clear examples of 'personality disorders'. In this chapter I have re-cast the traditional concept of 'personality disorders' as examples of *permanent* under-activity of the empathy circuit. It is impossible to establish if permanent really means permanent, since to test this would entail following individuals throughout their lives. Traits could instead be thought of as longer-term, and certainly more long-lasting, than short-term changes in states.

Before leaving the topic of Types B, P, and N, it is important step back and remember that people with these diagnosed personality disorders are not responsible for most of cruelty in the world. Indeed, as we've seen, people who are Type B may only hurt others when they are in the heat of a emotional crisis, and even then it may be through saying things that hurt another person, or because they hurt themselves (through suicide attempts or self-harm) causing their loved ones to suffer. People who are Type N may withdraw from others rather than being cruel towards them. The scientific lessons, however, for looking at empathy erosion in these three medical conditions is that they are revealing the workings of the empathy circuit in the brain.

But we have spent more than enough time probing the negative forms of zero degrees of empathy. Now I want to turn to the question of whether *all* forms of zero degrees of empathy are necessarily negative, and to the controversial idea that there is at least one way in which zero degrees of empathy can be positive.

4

When Zero Degrees of Empathy
is Positive

The three types of people whom we have met so far not only have zero degrees of empathy but are Zero-Negative. This is because there is nothing desirable about the state they have ended up in. If a cure came along for forms of Zero-Negative, this would be very welcome. In addition, so far I think one can replace the terms 'evil' and 'cruelty' with the term 'empathy erosion' in relation to the Zero-Negative forms. But in this chapter we discover that having zero degrees of empathy does not invariably lead someone to do awful things to others. Having empathy difficulties may be socially disabling but having empathy is not the sole route to developing a moral code and a moral conscience that leads the person to behave ethically. This is where we meet people who have zero degrees of empathy but who are Zero-Positive. It seems unthinkable, but bear with me.

Being Zero-Positive means that, alongside their difficulties with empathy, those affected have a remarkably precise, exact mind. They have Asperger Syndrome, a condition on the autistic spectrum. People with Asperger Syndrome are Zero-Positive for three reasons. First, in their case, their empathy difficulties are associated with having a brain that processes information in ways that can lead to talent. Second, the way their brain processes information paradoxically leads them not to be immoral, but super-moral. Finally, in people who are Zero-Positive, whilst their 'cognitive' empathy may be below average, their 'affective' empathy may be intact, enabling them to care about others. Let me make this more concrete by introducing you to Michael.

MICHAEL: ASPERGER SYNDROME

Michael is fifty-two years old. He has tried working in different jobs but keeps getting fired because he offends people by saying hurtful things. He claims he doesn't understand why people take offence at his remarks because all he does is speak the truth. If he thinks someone's haircut is ugly, he tells them. If he finds a conversation boring, he says so. If he thinks someone is wrong, he says so, in no uncertain terms. He confesses he doesn't really understand people, and he avoids social gatherings like parties where one is expected to make idle chitchat, as he can't see the point of such flighty, aimless conversation. To his mind, it leads nowhere and he has no idea how to do it. Conversations based around an issue where evidence can be marshalled in favour of a position are fine. Then he knows where the conversation is heading.

Other people often tell him that when he is trying to persuade them of the rightness of his position, he lectures *at* them rather having a sensitive dialogue. They often feel they are being pinned against the wall in such discussions, since he will not let go of a point until the other person concedes that he is right. But he finds other kinds of conversation stressful because it is so unpredictable. He has a long-suffering mother who can't get him to understand that there are other points of view besides his own. He asserts that he is right on everything he says because if he does not know about a topic, he remains silent on it. All facts for him are checked and double-checked.

He insists on everything being in its own place at home, with nothing being allowed to move to a new position unless *he* moves it there. His life operates by a system of rules that he imposes on his parents, rules designed to suit him. They complain that he has no idea how they feel, having to live within his rules. If his mother moves something small in the house, like an ornament from the mantelpiece to a bookshelf, he moves it back to its original position. If she wants to make a bigger change in the design of the house, such as moving the kitchen table over to the window, he will object and move it back. He likes to wear the same jeans, T-shirt, sweater and shoes every day, and eat the same foods every day. Indeed, until he was sixteen, all he ate was cornflakes. Personal hygiene has been a problem.

He always found social situations confusing and stressful – even as a child. He didn't play with other children in the playground, was never invited to their birthday parties, or picked to be on their team. He avoided the playground by going to the bottom of the playing field at primary school – alone – and counting blades of grass. In the winter when it snowed, he became obsessed with the structure of snowflakes, wanting to understand why each one was different. Other children in his class couldn't understand what he was talking about since in their eyes all snowflakes looked the same. Although the teacher had told all the class that every snowflake is unique, it seemed that he was the only person in the class who could actually *see* the small individual differences in the snowflakes. The other children in the class teased him, calling him 'snowflake brain'.

In secondary school he avoided social situations by going to the library and reading books about the history of the railways. He accumulated an enormous amount of information about the railway system but hardly spoke to a soul. He describes secondary school as if he simply walked the corridors for six years, from when he was twelve to when he reached eighteen years old. On a few occasions he was bullied, having his bag grabbed. When he chased after the other boys to get his bag back they taunted him, calling him 'nerdy', picked him up and put him in the school dustbin.

At university he studied mathematics, because he felt it was the only truly factual subject where things were either true or false. But he kept himself to himself. He hoped that all the years of loneliness during his school days would be behind him when he got to university, and he hoped that – for the first time in his life – he would feel accepted by others, fit in, and feel as if he belonged. Sadly, this didn't happen. Other students seemed to socialize together effortlessly, but he had no idea what to talk to them about. Their conversations still seemed like butterflies, flitting randomly from one flower to another, whereas he preferred conversations that progressed along logically linked linear paths, a series of facts or assertions that followed clearly from the previous step. When people suddenly switched topic or introduced humour or sarcasm or metaphor, or – even worse – body language, he was immediately lost. He noticed that 'other people seem to communicate through their eyes, not their words, and that they seem to know what each other means or what they are saying'. He hadn't a clue how they did this mysterious thing.

He dropped out of college because he was becoming depressed, even suicidal, as a result of his loneliness. He moved back to his parents' home aged twenty-two, spending all day alone in his bedroom, and refusing to even have mealtimes with his family. He is now unemployed because he finds interacting with people so stressful. He keeps himself to himself during the day. His dream is to live in a world without people, where he can have total control. Michael has zero degrees of empathy because, as he readily confesses, he has no idea what others are thinking or feeling, or how to respond to someone else's feelings. He has learned a few simple rules, such as 'When someone is upset, ask them if they want a cup of tea', or 'When someone is angry, apologize', but these rules don't seem to be very useful.

Michael's zero degrees of empathy does not lead him to do cruel things to others. He simply avoids other people. So here we see that although low empathy can increase the risk of hurting others, this is not inevitable. And Michael's empathy difficulties are about 'reading' other people (the 'cognitive' component in empathy). The other component of empathy (the 'affective' element) seems to be intact, because if he hears of someone suffering, it upsets him and he is the first to ask what can be done to prevent such suffering.

Alongside his difficulties with cognitive empathy, Michael's brain is always *busy* doing something else. If you watched Michael in his bedroom, you would see him obsessively drawing tiny patterns on squared paper, lines of different length that fill the page. He feels great pleasure when his patterns of lines produce the golden ratio ($1.61803\ldots$), which he explains is where the ratio of the sum of two numbers to the larger one (A+B/A) is *always* the same as the ratio between the larger and the smaller (A/B). He can't understand why everyone can't spot such simple, easy, patterns, as they recur in so many places – in nature, in architecture – and not just in maths. In his forties he developed an interest in becoming a bell-ringer. He not only hears the church bells ringing, but he notices every tiny pattern in the bells. He noticed that in Ely Cathedral they have five bells and that if you want all five bells to chime in a row, the longest they can be rung without repeating a row is 120 changes ($1\times2\times3\times4\times5$). In King's College (in my city of Cambridge), he noticed they have six bells and that they can have 720 changes (1×2×3×4×5×6). And in Great St Mary's Church (also in Cambridge) he noticed they had eight bells, so they could have 40,320 changes. He loves these timeless patterns.

The autistic brain

People who are Zero-Positive have autism spectrum conditions. They too show under-activity in most areas of the empathy circuit.[195, 196] When they have to read little stories to make judgements about a character's intentions, motives and state of mind, or when they have to read language to judge what a person intended, they show reduced activity in the dorsomedial prefrontal cortex (dMPFC).[197-199] When they are trying to infer what someone might think or feel while looking at photos of a person's eyes (decoding the facial expression around the eyes) they have great difficulties and show under-activity in the frontal operculum (FO), amygdala and anterior insula (AI).[80, 200, 201] Brain regions involved in processing gaze such as the posterior superior temporal sulcus (pSTS) are also atypical in autism.[202] This region also responds atypically in people who are Zero-Positive when they are looking at motion that seems animate (e.g., seeing moving dots that resemble the way a person would walk).[203] People who are Zero-Positive also show atypical amygdala activity when processing faces and emotion.[204-211] And the FO/IFG (inferior frontal gyrus) – part of the mirror neuron system – in individuals who are Zero-Positive shows reduced activity when asked to imitate other people's emotional facial expressions.[69, xxxiii]

Many of the early studies of 'mind-reading' or empathy in people who are Zero-Positive relied on verbal tests (e.g., interpreting stories, sarcastic comments, or labelling emotions). To bypass language, researchers have employed a clever task called the Social Attribution (or Animations) Test, where you get to watch an animation of geometric shapes moving about on the computer screen. Most people spontaneously anthropomorphize the movements of these geometric shapes, but people with autism and Asperger Syndrome are less likely to spontaneously interpret the movements of these animations in terms of intentions, thoughts and feelings. And when people with autism do this task in an MRI scanner they show the familiar under-activation of the dMPFC and right temporo-parietal junction/ posterior superior temporal sulcus (RTPJ/pSTS).[214–216]

In addition to difficulty in understanding others, people who are Zero-Positive also have difficulty understanding their *own* minds, a difficulty called 'alexithymia', which translates as 'without words for emotion'.[217–220] When people with autism are asked to rate how they feel after viewing emotionally charged pictures they show less activity during such 'emotional introspection' within a number of regions in the empathy circuit: the dMPFC, posterior cingulate cortex (PCC), and temporal pole.[221] This under-activity in the dMPFC is in the same area where people with autism show their difficulties in reading *others'* minds.[197, 199, 215, 216] So, the neural systems involved in mind-reading and empathy[18, 85] are all consistently under-active during empathy tasks in the autistic brain. The activity of the dMPFC and vMPFC at rest (in terms of its baseline activity)[xxxiv] is atypical in autism.[226, 227]

Tracking down reduced empathy in the autistic brain has been a major focus of my collaboration with talented former PhD student Mike Lombardo. He also found atypical neural activity when thinking about oneself in autism. The vMPFC responds most when information is self-relevant. Mike found that in people with autism the vMPFC does not distinguish between self and other in the usual way. Those who were most socially impaired showed the most atypical vMPFC response.[228] He also found that, when typical people think about themselves, the vMPFC is typically highly connected with other regions of the brain involved in sensory reactions (e.g., responding to touch), such as the somatosensory cortex. However, in autism the connections between the vMPFC and these lower level sensory regions are extremely reduced.

This fits with the results from a study by another talented visiting student, Ilaria Minio-Paluello, who came to Cambridge from Rome. Ilaria found that in typical people, when they viewed pictures of other people in pain (e.g., a hand being pricked with a needle), the sensori-motor cortex sends a signal to one's own hand to flinch, as if we feel what it's like to feel what the person in the picture is feeling. This sensorimotor response to others' pain was much lower in people with autism.[229] Thus, lower-level embodied processes affect empathy in autism, and higher-level self-reflection processes are also impaired in autism.

Mike also found a second region in the empathy circuit in people who are Zero-Positive that responds atypically to self-relevant information: the middle cingulate cortex (MCC). The MCC is usually activated during pain, but also when information is 'self-relevant'.[228] Atypical MCC activity is also found when people with autism play a game where they have to make decisions about how much money they want to trust to a second individual, and then wait to see if the other person will give money back to them or if they keep it all. Typically, the MCC is highly activate in such co-operative social interactions, particularly when someone is contemplating how much to trust the other person.[230] However, when people with autism play this game they don't activate the MCC when thinking what to do, perhaps because they find it hard to imagine how they will look to another person.[231, 232, xxxv]

So, just like those who are Zero-Negative, people who are Zero-Positive also show abnormalities in the same regions of the brain where empathy resides. So what makes Zero-Positive different?

Michael and other people with Asperger Syndrome have zero degrees of empathy, but they are Zero-Positive for two reasons. First, their empathy difficulties are largely restricted to the 'cognitive' component (also called 'theory of mind'). Their 'affective' empathy is frequently intact. We know this because – when it is pointed out to them that someone is upset – it often upsets them. Unlike people who are Type P, someone with Asperger Syndrome is very unlikely to hurt their pet. Indeed, the opposite is true. Many people with Asperger Syndrome rescue stray dogs or cats because they feel sorry for them and want to look after them. I have met people with Asperger Syndrome who have ended up with a large collection of stray dogs (a dozen or more) because of their strong affective empathy. In an imaginative study, Berlin neuroscientist Isabel Dziobek and colleagues found that people with Asperger Syndrome did not differ in how much concern they felt for people who were suffering, compared to typical individuals, even though they struggled to identify what others were feeling or thinking. This suggests people with Asperger Syndrome are the mirror image of those with Type P: Psychopaths have intact cognitive empathy but reduced affective empathy, whilst people with Asperger Syndrome have intact affective empathy but reduced cognitive empathy. The result is that people with Asperger Syndrome do care about others, whilst struggling to 'read' them. Those with Type P don't care about others, whilst 'reading' them with ease.[342]

The second reason why people with Asperger Syndrome are Zero-Positive is because, alongside their empathy difficulties, they *systemize* to an extraordinary degree. Systemizing is the ability to analyse changing patterns, to figure out how things work.[234, 235] Information changes happen in the world all day every day, and are either random or non-random. If change is non-random there is a pattern to it, and the human brain is tuned to notice patterns. Patterns are another word for repetition: we notice that a sequence of information has occurred before. How well we notice patterns is something that varies in the population. People with Asperger Syndrome have a brain that is exquisitely tuned to notice patterns.

Looking for rules is easy for Michael, but the social world, he has realized, doesn't seem to have rules. In contrast, the world of church bells is highly lawful and he has systemized sequences of sounds into repeating patterns so can predict the bells with precision. In his drawings he has systemized geometric patterns to predict how the lines will all join up to produce the ultimate, perfect shape. Michael's personality emerges more clearly when seen side by side with other people with Asperger Syndrome, because of their similarities. Kevin, another man with Asperger Syndrome, also finds social situations confusing, and he is never happier than when he goes out into his garden at midnight. At this quiet hour, when people are asleep, he can concentrate on the natural world (his particular interest is in the weather) and on his equipment (for measuring the weather). Each night he records information in his notebook: the date, temperature, rainfall and wind speed. He has hundreds of such notebooks, with thousands of recordings of these tiny patterns of information. Kevin systemizes the weather in an effort to predict it (at least in his garden). Figure 7 shows a photocopy of a page in one of his notebooks.

Figure 7: Kevin's notebook recording the weather

Daniel Tammet is another man with Asperger Syndrome. Like Michael and Kevin, he too grew up afraid of the playground at school, because he had no idea how to join in the games that other children played together so effortlessly. Some people compare him to the character that Dustin Hoffman played in the film *Rainman*, which was based on a real person (Kim Peek) with autism. This is because Daniel not only has a remarkable attention for detail but he has a seemingly infinite memory for detail too. In his case, he trained himself to memorize the number Pi (which you and I at best just know as 3.1415, to four decimal places) to 22,514 decimal places, earning himself the title of European champion in this memory feat.

Daniel systemizes numbers to an extraordinary degree, being able to multiply two six-digit numbers together as fast as a computer. Yet at the age of fourteen he told me he still did not realize you had to look at people when they talk to you, and had no friends.[236, 237] And there are others with autism or Asperger Syndrome who struggle to socialize, and who readily confess they have *no idea* how to empathize, but who have systemized art. Many tend to draw their own favourite images over and over and over again. Having mastered the technique they were aiming for, they then introduce systematic changes in their drawing, so that their art progresses from the simple to the magnificently complex. Lisa Perini, as a child living in Venice, Italy, only drew the letter W. Now, years later, her art has progressed to a remarkable degree.[238]

Derek Paravicini, blind and with classic autism, can anticipate and produce every note in a piece of music on the piano, whether it is blues or classical, if he has heard it just once. Despite his talent at systemizing music, his capacity to have a simple conversation is extremely limited, mostly restricted to repeating what the other person says. He rocks back and forth in repetitive ways when alone, and cannot function independently at all.[239] I met him when he came to play blues in Cambridge in 2006 with boogie-woogie master Jools Holland in a concert we hosted to fundraise for autism research, and he is a charming young man who amazed the audience with his ability to play any request anyone shouted out.

Finally, Peter Myers is a model builder in Yorkshire. Like the others with Asperger Syndrome, he keeps himself to himself, finding people confusing, and having trouble with conversation because he finds words ambiguous. Even the simple question of 'Where do you live?' he finds unclear, because it is not obvious whether the question is about a country, a town, a street, a house or a room. As a result, communication is an effort and is full of pauses. But this social disability emerges from the very same mind that produces artistic talent. He fills the page with tiny circles or squares in patterns, where each drawing is the product of thousands of hours of creating the same shape in slightly varied configurations. You can see an example of Peter's patterns in Figure 8.[240]

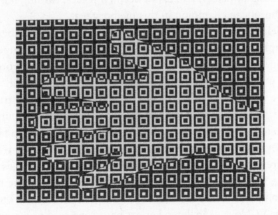

Figure 8: Art by Peter Myers

The puzzle is why these two seemingly different outcomes (low empathy alongside strong systemizing) should co-occur in one and the same individual. We will come back to possible solutions of this puzzle a little later, but, first, a word or two about 'systemizing' (since it lies at the heart of what it is to be Zero-Positive).

WHAT IS SYSTEMIZING?

The brain looks for patterns for different reasons. First, patterns enable us to predict the future. If the church bell chimes exactly ten times every Sunday morning at exactly 10 a.m., a mind that can systemize can then predict it will do so again this Sunday at exactly that time. Patterns in the church bells may not be a matter of life or death, but you can immediately see how such a general pattern-recognition system might have wide applicability – anything from predicting how prices vary in the market to how crops vary in different seasons. Patterns also enable us to figure out how things work by suggesting experiments we can perform, to confirm predictions. If I put a battery into my clock, the hands start to move. That's a nice simple example, but that same ability to spot patterns can enable you to figure out a new device that has no instruction manual, or enable you to repair a device that has multiple components. In each case, the trick is to manipulate one of these components at a time, and see what happens – what pattern is produced.

The other valuable thing about patterns is that they enable us to play with one variable at a time, to modify a system, thereby inventing a new one. If you make a canoe thinner, it moves through water faster. If you change the weight of an arrow, it can fly further, faster, and with greater accuracy. You can see that spotting such patterns is key to our ability to invent and improve.

Finally, spotting patterns provides us with direct access to the truth, since our predictions are either confirmed as true or false. The church bell either does or does not ring as predicted. Philosophers and theologians have long debated what we mean by truth. My definition of truth is neither mystical, nor divine, nor is it obscured by unnecessary philosophical complexity. Truth is (pure and simply) repeatable, verifiable patterns. Sometimes we call such patterns 'laws' or 'rules', but essentially they are just patterns. Sometimes the truth might not be all that useful (e.g., the British postman uses red elastic bands to bundle the envelopes), and sometimes the truth might be very useful (e.g., an extra chromosome 21 will switch a baby to develop Down Syndrome). Sometimes, the truth will reflect a natural pattern (e.g., left handedness is more common in boys than girls), and sometimes the truth will reflect a social pattern (e.g., in India you shake your head to show agreement). But it is the repeatability of a pattern that elevates it to the status of truth.

Stepping out of time

A fascination with patterns in their own right is what led humans to discover that, when a circle's diameter is 1, its circumference will equal Pi (or 3.1415 ...). Discovered in ancient Babylonia and calculated later with precision by Archimedes (c.287–212 BC), these early pattern-seekers had no idea that the beautiful pattern of Pi they had systemized would find a practical application almost 2,000 years later in Princeton, in physicist Albert Einstein's Relativity Theory. This was the human mind seeing the same patterns repeating in the world, irrespective of the time in which that human mind lived. Timeless patterns. The systemizing mind steps out of time to seek truths that are not tied to the present since, at a minimum, they have occurred in the past and have been confirmed to occur in the future. And, at least among the natural patterns, the truths may be eternal ones.

There are two ways to systemize. The first is by observation alone. We observe the changing data, and then look for a pattern in that data. (Is every seventh wave a big one? And does the big one always push the shells further up the beach?) Once we have identified a pattern, we then observe the data again to see if the rule we have formulated (big waves push shells further) is confirmed by new observations. We test if our prediction about the future is correct and true. The law is then maintained until new data comes along that does not fit the law, in which case the law is modified and subjected to more observation. This process can continue round and round in a loop, delivering truths as predictions are confirmed. In this first (observational) route to systemizing, the brain simply observes the input (counting the waves) and the output (the distance the shell is pushed) to identify the law (every seventh wave pushes the shell the furthest). Here, systemizing entails *input-output* relations.

The second way we systemize is by observation plus operation. We observe the data, and then perform some operation (manipulating one variable) and observe the effect of that operation. (Did the water rise when we dropped the rock into the bath?) What the brain is doing in this second route to systemizing is observing the input (noting the initial water level), performing an operation (dropping in the rock), and observing the output (noting the new water level). Here, systemizing entails *input-operation-output* relations.

We apply these two forms of systemizing to data from any domain that is systemizable. A system is anything that has lawful change or patterns. Both of these two forms of systemizing end up with rules of the form 'if p, then q'. A system might have one such rule or might have hundreds or thousands of such rules. A system could be a natural system (like ocean waves), a mechanical/man-made system (like an axe), an abstract system (like mathematics), a collectible system (like a shell collection), a motor system (like a dance technique), or even a social system (like a legal system). The same remarkable human ability to systemize has enabled humans to understand systems as small as cells or as extensive as the solar system, and to build systems as small as an equation or as extensive as a space satellite. Humans can not only figure out nature, but can harness such knowledge to make life easier and better for the rest of us, enabling us to send a text message from Nairobi to New York in seconds.

THE SYSTEMIZING MECHANISM

Let's call the 'Systemizing Mechanism' those parts of the brain that perceive patterns in changing information, enabling us to figure out how things work and to predict the future. The Systemizing Mechanism varies in the population. It has been studied using questionnaires

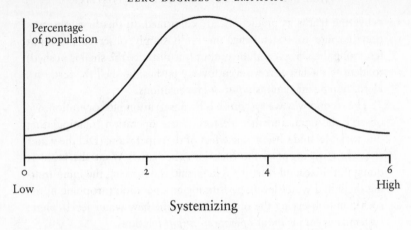

Systemizing

Figure 9: The systemizing curve

(the Systemizing Quotient, or SQ)[13, 241, 242] and tests of understanding mechanics.[243] Like the Empathizing Mechanism that we met in Chapter 2, we can glimpse that the Systemizing Mechanism also has six settings, a single mechanism tuned to different settings, from low to high, as shown in Figure 9.

People at **Level 0** notice no patterns at all. They might notice that the church bells chimed, but they wouldn't notice if they chimed in groups or be able to tell you how many bells there were. Their Systemizing Mechanism is tuned very low. Change just passes them by unanalysed. Since they are hardly interested in systemizing, they can deal with lots of change. Things can happen unexpectedly, interruptions can occur, or they can switch to a new activity even though they were in the middle of a task, and it doesn't bother them. They weren't looking for patterns, so they can deal with change.

People at **Level 1** notice easy patterns, such as strongly rehearsed ones (like even or odd numbers, or alphabetical filing systems, or people's birthdays), but find it almost impossible to figure out a novel system (like how to use a new appliance in the house). They would avoid subjects like mathematics at school, not being able to see the patterns. People at **Level 2** can see new patterns when they are pointed out to them but it is a struggle and they don't see these for themselves.

If asked to re-trace how the pattern was found, they would not be able to do this on their own. For example, having bought a new mobile phone, they might be able to follow how someone else manages to operate it but be unable to do so themselves.

People at **Level 3** can cope with simple, short systems, but may find longer, more complex ones challenging, while people at **Level 4** are quite adept at negotiating their way through systems. Without needing a manual, they will pick up a device and understand it through trial and error, and with confidence, quite quickly. More women are at Level 3 and more men are at Level 4. In their everyday lives, at these levels, people can still handle novelty, unpredictability and other people, without a second thought.

People whose Systemizing Mechanism is tuned at **Level 5** are likely to be interested in patterns and want to look for them in their daily life and work. People at this level gravitate towards the sciences, maths, music, technology and other analytical fields (such as linguistics, philosophy, or proof-reading/copy-editing), where searching for patterns is at the core. They try to create special environments (e.g., science labs) where they attempt to limit the amount of change, so they can analyse the effect of one variable at a time: removing *one* gene *at a time* from a mouse to see what happens, or looking at a chart of profits *one* month *at a time* to see what happens. They like to do *one thing at a time*. But they are not systemizing all day long, so when they socialize, or when things don't go as expected, they can deal with unsystematic environments. At Level 5 they like systems, so their lives are more orderly and routine, and they may even start each day by making a list of 'things to do today' and work their way through it. But they can still handle the unexpected.

Now we can get back to people with autism or Asperger Syndrome, because, according to this account, they have their Systemizing Mechanism turned all the way up to maximum (**Level 6**).[241] What is life like at Level 6? Here we discover individuals who have to systemize *every* moment of their waking lives. The only information they are interested in is patterned, systemizable information: repeating numbers, repeating musical sequences, repeating facts, repeating movements and actions.

Toxic change

Those at Level 6 can look at only one pattern at a time; the pattern is analysed one variable at a time. This search for predictable patterns comes at a terrible price: *anything* unexpected is, for them, toxic. A person walks into their bedroom unexpectedly while they are on the computer to do something ordinary (like open the curtains) and their stress levels go through the roof. Something that happens every Tuesday gets moved to a Wednesday and provokes a collapse. People at Level 6 are *hyper-systemizers*. These are the children who watch the washing machine going round and round and round for hours, and if pulled away to do something else will scream and resist change.

This is the world where Daniel Tammet lives, where Pi – even to 22,514 decimal places, is *always the same.* The sequence is comforting and reassuring, because it is 100 per cent predictable. People at Level 6 find change so difficult that they resist it at all costs, living in a totally controlled universe. The remarkable bonus of life at Level 6 is that you discover patterns that no one else notices. Such originality of perception can sometimes be called 'genius', which has been defined as looking at the same information that others have looked at many times before, and noticing a pattern than people have missed. The massive downside of life at Level 6 is that you can't cope with unexpected change.[244] These are the people that clinicians call autistic.

Consider two more unexpected consequences of life at Level 6. If your Systemizing Mechanism is turned up to the maximum, then you are interested in information only if it is *true*. Truth becomes the only thing that matters in the world. (Does a hydrangea planted in mildly acidic soil develop light blue petals, or in strongly acidic soil dark blue petals?) The truth matters at all costs. And this is not only in relation to the world of plants and rocks and machines, but also the world of people. Is my neighbour's behaviour consistent (i.e., true)? Do his words match his actions (are they true)?

People at Level 6 judge other people's behaviour as rigidly as they judge the behaviour of inanimate objects. The facts are either true or false. There is no room for shades of grey. People at Level 6 are so focused on the truth they become self-appointed moral whistle-blowers when someone breaks a rule, however minor. They accuse others of dishonesty if there is one tiny deviation between what they say and what they do. Whereas people whose Systemizing Mechanism is tuned to lower levels can deal with imprecision, at Level 6 it is precision that defines a system. At Level 6 there is no place for pretence, for figurative language, for vagueness, or for aimless chatting. Just facts.

It is this that at Level 6 creates this form of zero degrees of empathy. The world of people is a world dominated by emotions, where behaviour is unpredictable. How someone feels is not something that can be determined with precision. When we empathize it is because we can tolerate an inexact answer of what another person may feel. (Maybe she is a bit glum, or a bit angry.) And the world of feelings is unlawful. There are no black and white, consistent laws, unlike the world of physics or maths. Even worse, a social group means there are many different perspectives, not just a single objective view. Empathy involves simultaneously keeping track of different points of view and fluctuating emotional states in a social interaction, at high speed.

Here we see the link between the Systemizing and Empathizing Mechanisms: that if you have a highly tuned Systemizing Mechanism, you are less focused on unlawful phenomena such as emotions, in part because of a need for precision. A highly tuned Systemizing Mechanism turns out to be an additional route to zero degrees of empathy. Whereas if your Systemizing Mechanism is tuned low, you can tolerate imprecision, at Level 6 it is the opposite. Other people's behaviour is beyond comprehension, and empathy is impossible. When his colleague said to Michael the bell-ringer 'I have to go to my friend's funeral', Michael simply replied, 'OK. What time will you be back?'

Michael had no idea his matter-of-fact comment was insensitive. He had not intended to hurt his colleague but simply has no understanding of what might hurt another person's feelings. The downside of remarkable systemizing *is* a disinterest in unlawful phenomena, the clearest case of which is the world of emotions. So now we see why this form is Zero-Positive. Although the reaction to change as toxic and having zero degrees of empathy can be disabling, the love of patterns can lead to a mind that can see things that others miss. Indeed, people who were Zero-Positive in human history may have had such a clear perception of patterns that they contributed in remarkable and original ways to our discovery of physical, mathematical, chemical and other laws of the universe, as well as giving us great music and great art.[245]

JOE: CLASSIC AUTISM

At the outset of this book we defined loss of empathy as occurring when you treat a person as an object. But not everyone who treats others as objects *intends* to cause harm. For example, people with classic autism frequently treat others as objects, yet I would not want to group them with those who knowingly cause harm. Classic autism is the other major subgroup on the autistic spectrum, aside from Asperger Syndrome. I have argued that Asperger Syndrome is a case of Zero-Positive, but what about classic autism?

When I started my research into autism in the early 1980s I recall reading Baltimore child psychiatrist Leo Kanner highlighting this aspect of a boy in his clinic:

> When a hand was held out to him, so he could not possibly ignore it, he played with it briefly, *as if it were a detached object* . . .When he had any dealings with persons at all, he treated them, or rather parts of them, *as if they were objects* . . . It was as if he did not distinguish people from things, or at least did not concern himself about the distinction.[246]
> (italics added)

Now, some thirty years later, contemplating why people treat others as objects, I am drawn back to Kanner's clinical account. Many of these children treat others as objects, but fortunately it often does not lead to any major harm. They may ignore you, or appear oblivious of you, but there is no *intent* to do harm. Occasionally if you get in the way of their desires, you could of course be the victim of this self-centredness. For example, Michael Blastland writes about his own child with autism, Joe, that, 'When he wants something from me, I must suppose that I am Nature's universal vending machine, the great button to all desire, which if pressed frequently enough will provide.'[247]

How must it feel to be treated as if you were nothing more than a vending machine? At some level, all parents have had the experience that their child is simply treating them as if they will satisfy their every demand, as if the parent has no feelings or needs of their own. But, unlike a child with autism, most children also eventually detect that their parent is tired or upset or needs a rest. They know when to stop hassling. Some children are quicker at sensing their parent's feelings than others. Children with autism may sadly be blind to the very existence of other people's feelings, which can lead them to pursue their own desires regardless of the other person.

Michael and his son Joe were in a lift in the local shopping centre one day and a mother came in with her baby in a buggy. The baby started to cry and Joe – to everyone's shock – *punched* the baby to shut her up. Michael asks in his book:

> How do you explain to a complete stranger, this woman who cares about her baby more than anyone else in the world, that the pain that your son has just caused was not malicious, bad behaviour, but is because your 10 year old son has no idea that another person can suffer pain, or feel hurt by a punch?

According to Michael, Joe treats people, including this little baby, as one would an object. If the video player is too loud, there is a button to push to turn off the volume. If this baby is too loud, try hitting it to see if that turns off the volume. He describes how Joe hurled a toy brick at his sister with equally little awareness of her pain. But Blastland makes the point, and I agree with him, that Joe is no psychopath. His lack of awareness of others' feelings means he is not knowingly hurting them. The psychopath *is* aware that they are hurting someone because the 'cognitive' (recognition) element of empathy is intact in their case, even if the 'affective' element (the emotional response to someone else's feelings) is not. The person with classic ('low-functioning') autism may lack both of these components of empathy.

This illustrates how there are several ways to arrive at a point where one can treat a person as if they are a mere object. Joe may not have the evident 'savant' talents of some of the examples of Asperger Syndrome we have met in this chapter, but even in him, a boy with classic autism, one can glimpse his excellent attention to detail and love of patterns. Note too that pianist Derek Paravicini, who we encountered earlier, would be better described as having classic autism than Asperger Syndrome, since his language is limited mostly to repeating others' phrases and, aside from his clear musical genius, many of his self-help skills are quite limited and he remains totally dependent. The key point, however, is that, since there is no clear-cut point between autism and Asperger Syndrome, we should see them both as potential forms of Zero-Positive. I say *potential* because, if an individual has very severe learning difficulties, this may prevent their strong systemizing being expressed as talent.

WHERE WOULD WE BE WITHOUT ZERO-POSITIVE?

Zero-Positive is clearly a special case, where empathy is compromised but pattern-recognition and systemizing are enhanced. It prompts the question: where would *Homo sapiens* be if the Systemizing Mechanism had not been ramped up to high levels? Arguably we would not have as much (perhaps any) technological innovation and we would still be pre-industrial and pre-scientific. Strong systemizing allows humans alone to ask 'What if?' questions. I recently watched an episode of *Myth Busters* on the Discovery Channel, where people posed a 'What if?' question: what if we tried to raise a sunken boat just using ping-pong balls? Would the boat float to the surface? This is just the kind of ludicrous question that scientists enjoy asking. (The answer, by the way, is yes: it takes 25,000 empty ping-pong balls to float a 20-foot sunken boat.) Because humans can systemize, we have every kind of technology, from skateboards to iPhones. None of this would exist were it not for the ability we see writ large in those who are Zero-Positive. Society owes a special debt to those who have innovated in the fields of technology, music, science, medicine, mathematics, history, philosophy, engineering and other systemizing fields. The fact that they may be challenged when it comes to empathy is all the more reason to make our society more Zero-Positive-friendly.

So, we've seen that people who are Zero-Positive show empathy difficulties in their behaviour and that there are abnormalities in the empathy circuit in their brains. We've also seen that despite their low levels of empathy, this group of individuals do not for the most part act in cruel ways towards others. They are not like the Zero-Negative Type P, for example. That is because, even though most people may develop their moral code via empathy, in Asperger Syndrome affective empathy is intact whilst cognitive empathy is impaired, but in Type P the opposite profile is seen.[343]

Second, individuals who are Zero-Positive may have developed their moral code through intact affective empathy and through systemizing. They have a strong desire to live by rules and expect others to do the same, for reasons of *fairness*. James Blair was one of the first to show intact aspects of moral development in autism, but recent theories see super-developed moral codes in people with autism, being intolerant of those who bend the rules. People with Asperger Syndrome are often the first to leap to the defence of someone who is being treated unfairly, because it violates the moral system they have constructed though brute logic alone. As such, people who are Zero-Positive (those with Asperger Syndrome) are often among the law-enforcers, not the law-breakers. They warrant their 'positive' status because they systemize to an extreme degree and because their affective empathy is intact.

Interestingly, their parents show an echo of the same profile, raising the possibility that this is the result of genetics. For example, parents of children with autism show mild difficulties in reading the mind in the eyes of others. They also show a similar pattern of under-activity in regions of the empathy circuit in the brain when reading other people's emotions and thoughts from the face. Equally, siblings of children with autism exhibit intermediate levels of activation of the amygdala, between autistic and normal levels, during face-processing,[200, 209, 248, 249] implying genetic factors. Parents of children with autism are also overrepresented in systemizing professions, such as engineering.

We've hedged around the role of genetics, but it is now time to examine the role of genes in empathy head on.

5

The Empathy Gene

Why should one person be Zero-Negative and another Zero-Positive? At the psychological level, Zero-Negative occurs when an individual ends up all the way down at the far left end of the empathy curve, that curve of individual differences we encountered in Chapter 2. That tells us nothing about how they got there, a question related to the deeper level of causes. What we know is that the state of Zero-Negative can be caused by environmental neglect, such that the 'internal pot of gold' is depleted. But the existence of people who are Zero-Negative and who have *not* suffered neglect, together with the existence of people who *have* suffered neglect but who have excellent empathy, shows that such environmental factors may be neither necessary nor sufficient to cause zero degrees of empathy.

Take Zero-Negative Type P, for example: we saw in Chapter 3 that, while parental behaviour can be to blame, it cannot entirely explain the making of a psychopath, since among psychopaths parental style does not completely predict outcome.[250] That is, there are parents who used the empathic, non-authoritarian style of parenting, discussing things reasonably with their child, yet their child still turns out to be a psychopath. Equally, we all know individuals who have thrived despite growing up in difficult environments.

Dante Cicchetti grew up in the poorest, most dangerous neighbourhood of Pittsburgh yet has ended up as a professor of developmental psychopathology at the University of Minnesota. When I visited him at his research centre in the 1980s, he told me he was lucky to be alive. Most of his peer group from childhood were either in prison or dead, as a result of drugs, crime, or gang warfare. He is proof that growing up in what James Blair calls a 'dangerous and criminogenic' environment does not totally determine your outcome. In his studies he and his colleagues found that as many as 80 per cent of children who suffered abuse or neglect went on that to develop 'disorganized attachment'.[251] But clearly it takes more than a harsh environment to make a psychopath. There must be a genetic element.

In this chapter we therefore explore the new evidence that environmental factors interact with genes for empathy. The word 'interact' in the last sentence is, of course, key. I hope this book will not be misunderstood as arguing that empathy is wholly genetic, since genes always exist in an environment, and we have seen bucket-loads of evidence for the importance of early experience. Equally, I have to put the phrase 'genes for empathy' into quotes, since genes cannot code for a high level construct like empathy. Genes simply blindly code for the production of proteins, blissfully unaware of their ultimate long-range effects.

But in this chapter we examine evidence that some genes are *associated* with your score on various measures of empathy. Even with these caveats in place, some people will be alarmed at the very idea of genes for empathy because they fear the deterministic implications of such a view. I would remind those readers that genes alone are not solely deterministic, since the early environment is also. And I would ask them: should we simply sweep such genetic evidence under the carpet, just because it makes us feel uncomfortable? In the pursuit of trying to understand how human beings can end up doing awful things to each other, as we saw in Chapter 1 that they are capable of, we have to look at *all* the evidence, not just the bits that suit our world view.

The cause of the state of Zero-Positive is rather different. As we saw in Chapter 4, for such individuals, surfing *down* the empathy curve also means surfing *up* the systemizing curve. That is, they do not simply show zero degrees of empathy since at the same time they show high levels of systemizing. In their case, the genes that can leave them with zero degrees of empathy can also predispose them to extreme systemizing. We are therefore forced to conclude that *different* genes must be at work to produce Zero-Positive and Zero-Negative states. Before we look at specific genes that can deplete empathy to make someone Zero-Negative and the different genes that can deplete empathy to make someone Zero-Positive, we should first look at the biggest clue that such outcomes are genetic at all.

TWINS

If a trait or behaviour is even partly genetic, we should see its signature showing up in twins. The key comparison is between twins who are identical (monozygotic, or MZ) versus twins who are non-identical (dizygotic, or DZ). If the trait or behaviour in question does not differ much between MZ and DZ twins, then one is forced to conclude that genes play little if any role in the behaviour. This is because MZ and DZ twins are *genetically* quite different to each other: MZ twins are like genetic clones (they are genetically identical, so share 100 per cent of their genes), while DZ twins are genetically no different to any pair of siblings (they share on average 50 per cent of their genes). In contrast, MZ and DZ twins are *environmentally* quite similar to each other: they are the same age, typically growing up in the same family. Expressed differently, if you discover that the trait or behaviour in question shows a greater correlation among MZ twins than it does among DZ twins, then one can see that genes are at work.

Nearly all the studies of empathy in twins have found a greater correlation on empathy measures in MZ twins, compared to DZ twins.[252-254] As an example, the heritability of affective empathy (i.e., how much of the variation in affective empathy is genetic) has been estimated from a twin study to be 68 per cent. That's a lot. In contrast, one study looking at the heritability of 'theory of mind' (or cognitive empathy) found that MZ and DZ twins were quite similar,[255] suggesting environmental rather than genetic factors predominate. However, this was challenged by a later study.[256]

Estimates of precisely how big the environmental and the genetic contributions to empathy are vary depending on how empathy is measured. For example, some twin studies use questionnaire measures, whereas others use observational measures. In studies of very young twins, observational measures include asking a mother to fake getting her finger caught closing a suitcase while her child's reactions were filmed. Studies using this observational method among toddlers have shown a strong genetic component to empathy.[257, 258] Observational methods are better measures of 'affective empathy' (the responsive component) and may be suggesting that of the two main components of empathy (cognitive versus affective empathy) there may be a larger genetic contribution in the affective component. The phenomenon of finding it difficult to reflect and report on one's own feelings (alexithymia) also shows heritability from twin studies.[259]

Regarding Type Ps, a twin study that used the Psychopathic Personality Inventory (questionnaire) found specific scales (one called 'Machiavellian egocentricity', another called 'cold-heartedness') showed moderate heritability. In a UK study of twins, the callous and unemotional component of psychopathic tendencies at the age of seven showed even stronger heritability.[260, 261] Twins are not the only 'natural experiment' to glimpse the importance of genes, since the same clues are also seen in studies of children who have been adopted, again pointing to 'anti-social behaviour' being heritable.[262]

Adoption represents another opportunity for scientists to separate the effects of genes and environment, since, if a child – despite being raised in a different, genetically unrelated environment – ends up being more similar to their 'birth parents' than to their 'adopted parents', clearly genes are asserting their influence. Regarding twin studies of Type Ps, none of these shows 100 per cent heritability but the genetic component is nevertheless substantial (the largest estimate being about 70 per cent). This means there is still an environmental contribution to becoming a psychopath or developing some of the 'traits'. In the 'right' environment, someone with the genetic predisposition to psychopathy could show this behaviour.

Can we glimpse a genetic signature in Type N or Type B also? To date, there has not been a twin study of Type N – a gap in the literature that needs to be filled. Regarding Type B, family studies show that brothers, sisters and parents of borderlines are *ten* times more likely to be Type B themselves.[104, 263–269] Family studies (unlike twin and adoption studies) don't afford us the opportunity to separate environmental from genetic factors, so all we can conclude from family studies is that this form of Zero-Negative is 'familial' (it runs in families). However, a twin study of Type B indeed shows higher 'concordance' rates (35 per cent) among MZ than among DZ pairs (7 per cent). 'Concordance' is a fancy word for correlation and is used when you are counting how often it is the case that when one of the twins in a pair has a condition (e.g., Borderline Personality Disorder), the co-twin also has it. Although 35 per cent vs. 7 per cent may look like a small difference, this tells us that becoming borderline is actually strongly heritable – about 70 per cent of the risk for becoming borderline can be explained by genetic factors.[270, 271] So, despite the clear environmental influences (principally abuse and neglect), to become borderline requires the individual to have some genetic susceptibility in the first place.

What about the genetic signature of Zero-Positive? Family studies show that brothers, sisters and parents of people with autism or Asperger Syndrome (Zero-Positive) also show more than average levels of autistic traits.[200, 248, 249, 272–274] So we can glimpse that being Zero-Positive is familial. This is true both when you use assessment questionnaires such as the Empathy Quotient (EQ) and when you use psychological tests that measure emotion recognition from photographs, or when you measure brain activity during such tasks.[200, 249] Equally, twin studies of Zero-Positive show that MZ twins show a higher correlation than DZ twins do on measures of autistic traits.[275–277] Therefore, given all this evidence for genes for empathy, which genes determine whether you become Zero-Negative or Zero-Positive?

GENES FOR AGGRESSION

Some scientists have focused their study for empathy genes on those that affect the neurotransmitter serotonin. This is because too much serotonin in the synapse has been linked to aggression; and, equally, if you increase serotonin receptor activity, which clears serotonin from the synapse, this decreases aggression.[278] An example of a gene involved in clearing serotonin (and other neurotransmitters such as dopamine, noradrenaline and adrenaline) is the MAOA (monoamine oxidase-A) gene.

Now here's the interesting bit. There are several forms of this gene: one is called MAOA-L, because carriers of this gene produce low (L) levels of a key enzyme. The other form of the gene is called MAOA-H (because carriers produce high (H) levels of the same enzyme). Low levels of MAOA often mean high levels of neurotransmitters in the synapses. Not surprisingly, people with the MAOA-H form are less aggressive. People with the MAOA-L form are over-represented in warrior cultures (such as the Maori in New Zealand). For this reason, controversially, it has been called the 'warrior gene'. Controversially, because the Maori are not necessarily aggressive. It won't surprise you that this gene interacts with environmental factors. For example, Avshalom Caspi found that abused children with the MAOA-L form of the gene are more likely to develop anti-social behavioural problems compared to abused children with the MAOA-H form of the gene.[279, 280]

Animal research backs this up. Male mice with a deletion of the MAOA gene show more aggressive behaviour. In humans, male members of a Dutch family with a mutation of the MAOA gene showed high levels of aggression. And neuroimaging reveals the amygdala and anterior cingulate (two key regions in the empathy circuit) are smaller in MAOA-L carriers. Carriers of this version of the gene also show increased amygdala and reduced anterior cingulate activity when matching of facial expressions.[281, 282]

GENES FOR EMOTION RECOGNITION

We know that at least three genes can affect how your brain responds to emotional expressions and, as we have seen, emotion recognition is a key part of empathy. Depending on which version you have of the serotonin transporter gene (SLC6A4) affects how much your amygdala responds to fearful facial expressions (though not all studies confirm this).[283, 284] Genes that modulate the availability of other similar neurotransmitters (e.g., dopamine) also affect the amygdala's response to fear faces.[285–287] Recall that the amygdala is a key brain region in the empathy circuit. In addition, variations in the arginine vasopressin receptor 1A gene (AVPR1A) (which has been linked to autism) also influence how much your amygdala responds to faces showing fear or anger.[288]

The third gene was one we discovered in our lab, so let me tell you the story. Plenty of research shows that happy faces are rewarding to look at. Just as we like to look at food or beautiful landscapes, we find happy faces rewarding. This is true from infancy onwards, as demonstrated by the fact that the typical infant, from about eight weeks old, will smile at a happy face. (This is called the 'social smile'.) We also know that there are two key brain regions that are active when we are experiencing something rewarding: the striatum and the substantia nigra.[289, 290] So it comes as no surprise that these same brain regions are active when we look at happy faces.[291]

My former PhD student Bhismadev Chakrabarti wanted to know if there were genes that might influence how much your striatum responded to these happy faces. After all, we all know there are individual differences in how much we like to engage in people watching. So he chose a gene that was already known to be involved in how we respond to reward. It is called the cannabinoid receptor gene 1 (or CNR1). This gene is strongly expressed in the striatum, a reward system of the brain.[xxxvi] This gene gets its name from the drug cannabis, because its protein product is the main target for cannabis in the brain. Individual differences in this receptor are linked to how rewarding an individual will find cannabis. (Some people can smoke a joint and it will have no effects, others will find it pleasurable, and yet others will find it unpleasant.) We took a cheek swab from each of the people lying in the MRI scanner, from which we could extract their DNA, so as to test Bhisma's neat idea that the variation you have of this gene will affect how active your striatum is when you are looking at happy faces. Sure enough, this prediction was confirmed.

These three genes give us very clear examples of how your genetic make-up can change how your brain responds to other people's emotions.[291, 292] It is highly unlikely that these are the only genes that affect emotion recognition, but they are sufficient to show that there are genes involved in at least this aspect of empathy.

GENES ASSOCIATED WITH EQ

In 2009 Bhisma and I completed our second genetic experiment. We were interested to find out which genes were associated with individual differences on the Empathy Quotient (EQ). We had hundreds of people from the general population take the EQ and, as we saw in Chapter 2, we observed the bell-curve (or 'normal') distribution – some scoring low, some scoring medium, and some scoring high on empathy. This is termed 'normal' because these individual differences are just what you expect to see in any population, just as you see individual differences in height. The big question was: if we picked some plausible 'candidate' genes, would variations in any of these genes be associated with variation in EQ scores?

The way we went about testing for empathy genes is worth a short digression, since gene-hunting is a risky business. Given that there are estimated to be 30,000 genes in the human genome, gene-hunters have two strategies available to them: a 'whole genome scan' (i.e., to test all 30,000 genes), which is a costly business; or test plausible 'candidate' genes, which is slightly more affordable (since you pay per gene per person). Essentially, this choice of strategy boils down to the difference between a fishing expedition where you have no particular hypothesis about where the fish will be (so you drop your line in 'blind' at regular points all along the river), versus a highly directed 'hypothesis-driven' approach (where you know that the fish are likely to gather at a very specific point in the river). We chose this candidate gene, hypothesis-driven approach.

The next question was which candidates to choose. It is a high-risk strategy since, if you choose correctly, you can really strike lucky. But, if you happen by pure misfortune to have chosen incorrectly, all you have to show for your troubles are a bunch of non-significant (and therefore unexciting) results. Bhisma and I sat down to plan our strategy. I was very keen on a group of genes involved in the sex hormones (testosterone and oestrogen) and persuaded Bhisma this was worth a try. My main reason was that empathy shows clear sex differences at the level of psychology. Girls and women score high on the EQ compared to boys and men, for example – a result that is found across different cultures and which I discussed at length in my last book *The Essential Difference*.[12, 15, 17, 293]

My second reason was that empathy shows clear sex differences at the level of the brain: women show more activity in many areas within the empathy circuit while reading emotional expressions in faces,[249] and a recent study of structural differences between male and female brains indicated that many of the brain regions that differ between the sexes include the amygdala and the 'mirror neuron system', which overlaps with parts of the empathy circuit.

I had one more reason for wanting to test the genes that regulate the sex hormones. For the last ten years we have been following a group of about five hundred children in Cambridgeshire, whose mothers had had amniocentesis. This is where a long needle is introduced into the mother's womb during pregnancy to draw off some of the amniotic fluid, a procedure carried out for clinical reasons. We had asked these mothers for permission to measure the testosterone in the amniotic fluid, the so-called male hormone because males produce much more of it than females do. We found that the less testosterone produced by the foetus ('foetal testosterone') before birth, the higher the score on the child version of the Empathy Quotient (EQ). So it seemed that this sex hormone might be involved in shaping the empathy circuit of the developing human brain.[xxxvii]

For all these reasons, we selected genes known to be involved in sex steroid hormones.[xxxviii] We expanded our team to bring in two world experts in medical genetics research, Lindsey Kent and Frank Dudbridge. Bhisma wanted us to include a second group of genes that we loosely called 'social-emotional behaviour' genes. This was to follow up on the CNR1 gene, but also to test the idea that there may be other genes that influence how drawn you are to other people. One such gene related to another hormone, oxytocin. Oxytocin has had a lot of press interest since it was discovered that males in one species of vole (a furry rodent) are less sociable (and likely to be polygamous) than males in another species of vole, who are more sociable (and likely to be monogamous). These two species are largely identical apart from a dramatic difference in the expression of oxytocin and vasopressin in the brain.[296-298] Oxytocin also hits the news a lot because, if you inhale it through your nose so that it goes straight into your brain, or if you inject it into your blood, it improves your score on tests of emotion recognition and empathy.[299, 300]

In the popular press oxytocin has a variety of names. It is sometimes called the 'love hormone' because we release it during intimate physical contact, including orgasm. It is also sometimes referred to as the 'trust hormone' because if you boost your oxytocin levels you tend to be more generous towards others, as measured by how much money you would be willing to lend a stranger.[301, 302] And, finally, it is also sometimes referred to as the 'attachment hormone' because it is released by new mothers during breast-feeding, promoting that well-being feeling that drives mothers to fall in love with their infant, and vice versa.[303] So we tested genes such as those involved in its synthesis and the receptors of oxytocin, as well as the closely related peptide hormone arginine vasopressin (AVP).

Finally we selected a set of candidate genes involved in what we loosely called 'neural growth', simply because studies of the brain in Zero-Positive individuals (with autism and Asperger Syndrome) had revealed atypical patterns in how the nerve cells (neurons) are wired up and how fast the autistic brain grew in early postnatal development.

We waited with bated breath while the genotyping took place, and wondered whether the substantial time and money we had invested would all be to no avail. Imagine our excitement when the results came through: of the sixty-eight candidate genes we tested, four of them showed a *strongly* significant association with the EQ! One of these genes was in the sex steroid group (CYP11B1). A second gene was in the group related to social-emotional behaviour, called WFS1.[xxxix] The third and fourth genes associated with EQ were in neural growth group: NTRK1[xl] and GABRB3.[xli]

So, all in all, we had found four genes for empathy.[304] This of course was only a first step, since it is a big jump from finding genes to understanding how their functions have an impact on empathy. But a start is a start.

GENES ASSOCIATED WITH AUTISTIC TRAITS

Bhisma and I had taken the precaution of asking our volunteers from the general population to fill in not only the EQ, but also the Autism Spectrum Quotient (AQ), a measure of how many 'autistic traits' you have. This is because our earlier studies had shown this too to be replete with individual differences: some people score low, having few autistic traits, others score in the average range for the population, and yet others score high, even though they don't have a diagnosis of any kind. As we saw in Chapter 4, autistic traits are not all negative.

While reduced empathy can cause social difficulties, a remarkable attention to detail and an ability to concentrate on a small topic for hours, to understand that topic in a highly *systematic* way, can be positive, and can lead the individual to blossom in certain fields, despite their relative difficulties with empathy and socializing. And if you're blossoming in a non-social academic field (such as mathematics or computer science, engineering or physics) or in a non-social practical line of work (such as car maintenance, map-making, or railway timetabling) or form of art or craft (such as drawing, model-building, or design), you may find a niche and get by without a diagnosis. For these reasons, we might find genes related to autistic traits in our general population.

So, would any of our candidate genes also show a significant association with the AQ? There were four more genes that were only associated with AQ. These included one of the neurologin genes (NLGN4X), one of the homeobox genes (HOXA1) that regulate brain patterning, and ARNT2 (a gene involved in neurogenesis). It also included a monoamine oxidase gene (MAOB), similar to the gene we discussed earlier.

Finally, we looked at whether any of our candidate genes were strongly associated with being Zero-Positive (having a diagnosis of Asperger Syndrome), and were very excited to find six genes that were. These included three sex steroid genes: ESR2 (one of the receptors for oestrogen), CYP17A1 (abnormalities in which cause irregularities of the menstrual cycle in women), and CYP11B1 (one of the genes that catalyzes the production of testosterone from cholesterol, and has also been linked to empathy). It also included the oxytocin gene (OXT), as well as ARNT1 and HOXA1 (also linked to empathy).

This told us that while some genes were influencing just EQ alone, others were influencing just AQ alone, Zero-Positive states alone, or several of these. Such genetic work opens up more questions and avenues of research.[xlii]

STEPPING BACK

The genes we have discussed in this chapter are by no means the complete list of genes that will turn out to play a part in empathy. There are without doubt more to be discovered, and some of the above may not stand the test of time in terms of independent replication. But the list above is sufficient to show that genes for empathy and for some forms of both Zero-Negative and Zero-Positive are being discovered.

However, it is important to reiterate the caveats at the start of this chapter. While it is tempting to blame the cause of having zero degrees of empathy on either genes or environment, it is clearly a mix of factors. For example, babies who had difficult births where they suffered anoxia (lack of oxygen) have a higher risk of developing Conduct Disorder, delinquency, or of being violent in adulthood. Boys with minor physical anomalies (e.g., having low-hung ears) have a higher risk of later becoming violent offenders, especially if they live in an unstable home.[306] The low-hung ears can occur for genetic reasons, or because the mother had bleeding and infection during pregnancy, indicating that the baby was not in the best of health during early pregnancy. These increase a child's risk of being violent (and therefore being low in empathy) if they coincide with instability in the family environment. For example, in a Danish study 4 per cent of boys had both a difficult birth and maternal rejection, yet these boys committed 18 per cent of the violent crimes in adulthood.[307] Once again, we see the complex interplay of biological factors (in this case birth trauma) and psychological factors (in this case a depleted 'internal pot of gold').

DO OTHER ANIMALS HAVE EMPATHY?

And we can step back from humans, too, to ask if other animals have at least in simpler form some of the precursors of empathy. They should have if empathy is in part genetic, since typically intermediate forms of evolved traits can be seen across the animal kingdom. Emory University primatologist Frans de Waal[308] has argued that humans are not the only species to be capable of empathy, though he acknowledges that in humans it may have evolved to a higher level than that seen in other species. But, in his view, the precursors of empathy are evident in a number of behaviours. First, some monkeys and other animals will *share food* with other members of their own group. Why should they do this if they were entirely selfish?

Figure 10: Capuchin monkeys share food. They are more likely to choose a token that earns them and another monkey a slice of apple if they know the other monkey, than to choose a token that earns them a slice of apple alone.

It could be argued that this form of apparent altruism is in fact driven by genetic relatedness – that, in helping members of your group who may be your cousins and who therefore share some of your genes, you are ultimately helping to protect copies of your genes (in others) that may enable their host to survive and reproduce, thereby perpetuating your (shared) genes. In a recent experiment at Emory University, when capuchin monkeys were given the choice to have food alone or food when another monkey was also given food, they chose the social option if they knew the other monkey. This suggests that food sharing is not just confined to genetically related members of your group – it seems to extend to acquaintances too (see Figure 10).[309]

Secondly, there are other examples of animals of the same species *helping* each other, not just around sharing of food. For example, some chimpanzees have been observed to help each other to climb over a high wall. These are compelling examples of the ability to read each other's needs and goals. Thirdly, de Waal observed that after monkeys or apes fight, the loser is often shown *consolation* by other members of the group. As he licks his wounds, another animal will come over and touch him gently or even put an arm around the defeated animal, as if to offer comfort. This use of touch strongly resembles what we would do to a person in discomfort, and, at risk of anthropomorphism, we might interpret it as an appropriate emotion to someone else's emotional state – in short, empathy.

Finally, monkeys and apes show plenty of evidence that they can read the facial expressions or vocalizations or body posture of another member of their species. For example, Northwestern University clinical psychologist Susan Mineka and her colleagues famously showed that young monkeys could learn to fear a snake if their mothers showed fear in their face and voice,[310] and Wisconsin University psychologist Harry Harlow also found that monkeys reared in isolation and then reintroduced into a social group tended to react as if a friendly approach by a fellow monkey was an aggressive approach, while those reared by their mothers and with their siblings could clearly distinguish between another animal's 'intentions' (to be friendly or aggressive).[311]

In two remarkable early studies, if a rat learns that pushing a bar will lower another rat who has been suspended in the air onto the ground, the rat will press the lever.[312] That's in rats, which are meant to lack empathy! And in our closer relatives, Northwestern University primatologist Jules Masserman and colleagues showed in 1964 that rhesus monkeys that are trained to pull a chain to get food will refuse to do so if pulling the chain also means another monkey is given an electric shock. It was as if they refused to profit at the expense of another monkey's pain.[313] One can quite see why some people believe other animals, including monkeys and apes, have some level of empathy.

However, there are clearly limits to empathy in other species. Chimpanzees can, for example, fight 'deadly turf wars' to expand their territory, in which large groups send out 'patrols to strategically kill rivals' before moving into the new territory.[xliii] Such 'cruelty' is of course common in other species as well as our own. As another example, whereas even human toddlers will use their index finger to point to things, to share attention with another person, getting them to look at something interesting or relevant to the other person, pointing is not seen in other species. Nor do other animals convincingly engage in deception, suggesting they do not think about another animal's thoughts, even if they can respond to their emotions.[314]

And, in a striking example from vervet monkeys, mother monkeys that are swimming across a flooded rice field to get to dry land might have their infant monkey clinging to their furry underbelly. While the mother's head is above water, many are blissfully unaware that their infant's head is underwater, so that when they arrive safely at the other side of the field, tragically their baby has drowned. This vividly underlines how monkeys may literally not take another animal's different perspective into account, with hard-hitting consequences and despite the impact this will have on the survival of their own genes. Clearly, whatever glimmerings of empathy we can discern (or imagine we discern) in other species, the level of empathy that humans show is qualitatively different to that seen in any other species.

6

Reflections on Human Cruelty

My aim in this book has been to re-stimulate discussion on the causes of evil, by moving the debate out of the realm of religion and into the realm of science. I have done this not because I have a Dawkinsian anti-religion agenda. On the contrary, I think religion has an important place for individuals and communities, whose identities are tied up with such cultural traditions, rituals and practices. But religion has been singularly anti-enquiry on the topic of the causes of cruelty. For most religions, the existence of evil is simply an awkward fact of the universe, present either because we fall short in our spiritual aspirations to lead a good life or because such forces (e.g., the Devil) are in constant battle with divine forces for control over human nature.

Extremes of evil are typically relegated to the unanalysable ('Don't ask why such things happen. It's just the nature of evil'); the reasoning becomes frustratingly circular ('He did x because he is truly evil'); and these extremes are sometimes even used to reinforce our belief in God ('God wants to test us'). If I have an agenda it is to urge people not to be satisfied with the word 'evil' as an explanatory tool, and, if I have moved the debate out of the domain of religion and into the social and biological sciences, I will feel this book has made a contribution.

But such an aim is rather broad, and of course I had some more specific aims in this book. In particular, I hope it has introduced ten new ideas into the debate. Here they are in brief:

First, we all lie somewhere on an *empathy spectrum* from high to low. Part of what science has to explain is what determines where an individual falls on this spectrum. I have pointed to some of the genetic, hormonal, neural and environmental contributory factors, and my list is not comprehensive because not all the evidence is yet available. The list at least shows how we can go about adding to such evidence.

Second, at one end of this spectrum is *zero degrees of empathy*, and we can classify zero degrees of empathy into Zero-Negative and Zero-Positive forms. The three major sub-types of Zero-Negative are Types P, N and B. Of course these are not all the sub-types that exist. Indeed, alcohol, fatigue and depression are just a few examples of states that can temporarily reduce one's empathy, and schizophrenia is another example of a medical condition that can reduce one's empathy. More sub-types will need to be characterized, but this list at least initiates the process. Critics may reasonably ask: surely there is nothing new about Types P, N and B? Haven't we have known for at least half a century about these three personality disorders? I would reply that this is precisely the problem. The traditional classification system has categorized these three types as *personality disorders*, overlooking what they all share: that they are all forms of zero degrees of empathy. Thus, their existence is not new, but in this book I have suggested we subtly shift how we think about them. At the surface level, they can properly still be viewed as personality disorders. But we can now go beyond the surface level, to link all three to a common underlying mechanism: empathy.

Third, whatever route one takes to zero degrees of empathy, the normative brain basis of empathy (the *empathy circuit*) will be atypical at zero degrees of empathy. In Chapter 2 we saw the ten brain regions that make up this circuit, and in Chapter 3 we saw how these were indeed (in different combinations) atypical in the Zero-Negative brain types. Calling them personality disorders doesn't guide us as to where to look in the brain for their basis. Calling them Zero-Negative guides us precisely where to look in the brain for their basis. At the intersection of Types N, B and P (see Figure 6, page 31) are this set of ten brain regions. In this sense, psychiatry could lump together a range of apparently separate medical conditions as Zero Degrees of Empathy, changing the way we classify and diagnose.

Fourth, *treatment* of zero degrees of empathy should target the empathy circuit. Treatments for empathy might include educational software such as the *Mindreading* DVD (www.jkp.com/mindreading) or *The Transporters* children's animation (www.thetransporters.com) we created for people with autism spectrum conditions.[315, 316] The former was designed for all ages, so lends itself to a trial with adults who are Zero-Negative. The promising findings of oxytocin nasal inhalation spray boosting empathy in typical individuals and in people with autism[299, 317] suggests this too could be tried in people who are Zero-Negative. Forms of role-play that involve taking the victim's perspective may also be worth trying. Calling them personality disorders leads to debates about whether one can really change someone's personality, especially if personality is defined as an enduring, fixed set of traits. Calling them Zero-Negative opens up new avenues for intervention.[xliv]

Fifth, Bowlby's remarkable concept of early secure attachment can be understood as an *internal pot of gold*. While not a new idea, it is a new term, and it is a message that I never tire of hearing, since when we fail to nurture young children with parental affection we deprive them of the most valuable birthright we can give them, and damage them almost irreversibly. Such effects are not always evident in childhood or even adolescence and young adulthood, but can come back to bite the individual in mid-life, like a lead boomerang in the back of the head. Certain forms of Zero-Negative only surface under the stresses of environmental triggers in later life, such as when becoming a parent oneself. One reason I think we must continue to remind each new generation of parents of the importance of the internal pot of gold is that it represents one avenue of intervention, to change the course of an individual life from Zero-Negative to a healthy, empathic individual.

Sixth, there are *genes for empathy*. As we saw in Chapter 5, environmental triggers interact with our genetic predispositions, and scientists are starting to discover particular genes that in far-reaching ways influence our empathy. I re-state that these are *not* genes for empathy per se but are genes for proteins expressed in the brain that – through many small steps – are linked to empathy. These steps are still to be clarified, but we can already see from statistical analyses that genes exist that are *associated* with empathy. By itself, this discovery will upset those who want to believe empathy is wholly environmental, and to those people I would say that the argument in this book is in fact a modest proposal: namely, that both biology and environment are important. Indeed, the idea that empathy is wholly environmental is a far more extreme and radical position to adopt.

Seventh, while most forms of zero degrees of empathy are clearly negative, one is (surprisingly) *positive*. The existence of Zero-Positive equates with what psychiatry calls autism spectrum conditions, and implies that at least one form of zero degrees of empathy may have been positively selected in evolution because it goes hand-in-hand with strong systemizing. A second reason why autism spectrum conditions can be thought of as Zero-Positive is because their empathy difficulties are largely restricted to the cognitive component (or theory of mind), leaving their affective empathy relatively intact. This gives them a basis for developing a feeling of caring about others, unlike individuals who for example are Type P. Some parents may of course object that classic autism has little to recommend it, and it is true that the co-existing conditions of severe learning difficulties or language delay or epilepsy or self-injury are indeed disabilities that do not confer anything positive to the individual. But these are co-existing conditions and do not define the autism spectrum per se. When these are stripped away, as in Asperger Syndrome, we see individuals who, despite their difficulties with cognitive empathy are often caring individuals and who are strong systemizers, which can be remarkably positive.

Eighth, Zero-Positive is the result of a mind constantly striving to *step out of time*, to set aside the temporal dimension in order to see – in stark relief – the eternal repeating patterns in nature. Change represents the temporal dimension seeping into an otherwise perfectly predictable, systemizable world, where wheels spin round and round and round, levers can move only back and forth, or church bells peal in beautifully mathematical patterns. After many such repetitions one loses any sense of time because events are the same each time. Such a state is what I assume people with autism are referring to when they talk of 'stimming'. They may become aware of the dimension of time only during events that contain novelty and which therefore violate expectations.

Ninth, the Zero-Positive mind finds *change toxic*. When such predictable patterns are interrupted, for example by the existence of another person who might perform an unpredictable action (e.g., saying something unexpected, or just moving), for someone with Zero-Positive this can be aversive and even terrifying. Hence they typically resist change at all costs. Classic autism is such a case of total resistance to change, a retreat into a perfectly systemizable – and thus perfectly predictable – world.

Finally, empathy itself is the *most valuable resource* in our world. Given this assertion, it is puzzling that in the school or parenting curriculum empathy figures hardly at all, and in politics, business, the courts or policing it is rarely if ever on the agenda. We can see examples among our political leaders of the value of empathy, as when Nelson Mandela and F. W. de Klerk sought to understand and befriend each other, crossing the divide in Apartheid South Africa, but the same has not yet been achieved between Israel and Palestine,[318] or between Washington and Iraq or Afghanistan. And, for every day that empathy is not employed in such corners of the world, more lives are and will be lost.

Many questions remain. First off, if different forms of zero degrees of empathy all involve the abnormalities in the empathy circuit, why do different individuals end up with one form or another? One way to answer this is to compare and contrast the different forms of zero degrees of empathy in terms of their overlapping but unique profiles. Table 1 does this at the psychological level, fractionating each one in terms of whether both aspects of empathy are impaired or intact (the cognitive and affective components) and whether systemizing is impaired or intact. A similar exercise will one day be possible in terms of each of the ten brain regions, each of the 'empathy genes', and each of the environmental triggers. Zero-Positive splits into at least two subgroups and this must also be because there are causal factors (again genetic and/or environmental) underlying language development and IQ, the two key dimensions distinguishing these two subgroups (classic autism vs. Asperger Syndrome). But Table 1 gives an illustration of how an answer will be found.

Second, are there *other* forms of zero degrees of empathy? One way to answer this question is to pick a clear example of a different form that we have not yet discussed, to show that the list is far from complete. For example, psychiatrist Professor Janet Treasure at London's Institute of Psychiatry has suggested that at least some cases of anorexia may not just be an eating disorder but a form of Asperger Syndrome. Her observation built on earlier ones by Swedish psychiatrist Chris Gillberg.[320] Almost as soon as she pointed this out, many could see the importance of this theoretical shift in view: although in individuals with anorexia we are struck by their severe weight loss

Table 1: Distinct profiles of the empathy disorders

	Cognitive Empathy Positive (CE+)	Cognitive Empathy Negative (CE−)	Affective Empathy Positive (AE+)	Affective Empathy Negative (AE−)	Morality Positive (M+)	Morality Negative (M−)	Systemizing Positive (S+)	Systemizing Negative (S−)
Zero Negative								
Type P (Psychopathic)	√			√		√		
Type B (Borderline)		√		√				
Type N (Narcissistic)				√				
Zero Positive								
Classic Autism		√		√	√		√	
Asperger Syndrome		√	√				√	

and their restricted food intake, regarding this as *primarily* an eating disorder may place too much importance on surface features.

A characteristic of anorexia that many clinicians and parents instantly recognize is the self-centred lack of empathy, even though this is not one of the diagnostic criteria. While her (although on occasions his) parents are beside themselves with worry as their child continues down the potentially fatal path of self-starvation, the girl herself may stubbornly insist that she is happy with her body shape and weight. She may insist on eating separately from the rest of the family, more concerned with counting calories and weighing food to the nearest milligram than in fitting in with the family group. This inability to see another point of view looks a lot like another form of zero degrees of empathy.

Traditionally psychiatry has viewed individuals with anorexia as showing 'a total preoccupation with food and diet', and has viewed individuals with autism as showing 'unusually narrow and restricted interests and extreme repetitive behaviour', assuming these were totally different sorts of phenomena. According to this new view, traditional psychiatry may be failing to see that both of these entail excellent attention to detail, strong systemizing, and an extreme narrow focus or 'obsession'. Seen through this new lens, the individual with anorexia is 'resistant to change' in the same way that someone with autism is. The fact that, in one case, the repetitive behaviour is in the domain of food and body shape while, in the other, it is in the domain of toy-car wheels spinning round and round may be irrelevant. On this argument, at least one subgroup of anorexia individuals may benefit from being reconceptualized as not just having an eating disorder (which they clearly do), but also as being Zero-Positive. This has very different treatment implications.

So, although this book has considered three forms of Zero-Negative, there are undoubtedly others. Another example would be people with specific delusions, like erotomania,[xlv] where someone believes that another person is in love with them when they are not. This was famously described in Ian McEwan's novel *Enduring Love*, where the person's delusion prevents them from being able to be sensitive to the other person's feelings. They might stalk them and try to control them, which is clearly unempathic.

My next question is whether someone can have more than one form of zero degrees of empathy. The answer to this is a definite 'yes'. The idea that there are different forms of Zero-Negative, and that these are distinct from Zero-Positive, should not be taken to imply that a single individual can only have one of these types. Certainly, I have met individuals who are both Zero-Positive and Type B. Other clinicians may well know of individuals who are both Type P and Type N, etc. But the fact that one can have one Type without the other is evidence of their independence, and an argument for making these distinctions.

So many questions remain. Here's another: does someone who commits murder *by definition* lack empathy? I want to tell another story to help us see why the profession of psychiatry itself needs to rethink the importance of empathy.

RETHINKING PSYCHIATRY

I found myself sitting next to expert forensic psychiatrist Dr Neil Hunt at a supper in St John's College in Cambridge the other night. He told me he was the psychiatrist called out to assess Rekha Kumari-Baker, the mother who stabbed her two daughters to death in the local village of Stretham on 13 June 2007. She explained in her court trial how she had become jealous of her ex-husband because, even though they were divorced in 2003, he had a new partner and she did not. She wanted to hurt her ex-husband and thought this would be the way to shatter his happiness.[321]

Neil had to determine if Rekha was suffering from any mental illness. He decided that, in his opinion, she was not. According to DSM-IV (the *Diagnostic and Statistical Manual*, 4th edition),[131] the book that sits on the desk of every psychiatrist throughout the world and that psychiatrists consult to classify all 'mental illnesses', she did not fit into any of the available categories. Although she had felt some depression when she split up from her lover, *at the time of the assessment* (the day of the crime) she showed no signs of depression, anxiety, psychosis, long-standing personality disorder, or indeed any of the 297 disorders listed in DSM-IV. Therefore, according to Neil and according to how psychiatry conceptualizes people, *she was not mentally ill*. DSM-IV can only put people into one of two over-arching categories: mentally ill, or mentally normal. So, by implication, if Rekha did not fit into any of the DSM categories, despite killing her two children, she must be normal. I'm sure you can see the common-sense contradiction here, and why I take issue with current psychiatry.

Of course, some might argue that another reason for deciding she was not mentally ill would be that, if Neil had said she was mentally ill, this would have given Rekha grounds for pleading 'diminished responsibility', and thus have the crime viewed as manslaughter rather than murder. In the end, the court accepted Neil's expert opinion and found her guilty of murder, sentencing her to thirty-three years in prison. (She will thus not be eligible for parole until 2040, when she will be seventy-two years old.)

While I agree this is the kind of sentence that fits the horrific crime, I do think it shows up the limitations of DSM-IV, and therefore of psychiatry, if the prevailing diagnostic system categorizes this woman as normal. Sentencing is a matter for the court and ultimately the judge. Diagnosis is a matter for the doctor, in this case a psychiatrist. The two are rightly kept rigorously separate. That Rekha didn't fit into any existing psychiatric category is not Neil's fault. It is the fault of psychiatry itself.

In my view (and, I would venture, the commonsense view), anyone who can stab their own daughter with the intent to kill is – *by definition* – not psychologically normal. *By definition* they lack empathy, at least at the time of the crime. Even if Rekha had previously shown normal empathy, it must be the case that, *at the very moment* she was climbing the stairs holding a kitchen knife, with the intent of stabbing her children, and *at the very moments* she plunged the knife into her children, she lacked empathy. Her empathy must have gone, just not been there. To me, the obvious conclusion is that the medical and psychiatric classification system is crying out for a category called 'Empathy Disorders', which is where Rekha would have naturally fitted. Even if she did not show the long-standing empathy impairment that would be required for a diagnosis of a personality disorder, at the very least she must have had a transient or long-standing 'empathy disorder'. The problem, though, is that the category of 'empathy disorder' does not exist in DSM-IV, and as far as I know there are no plans for such a category to be created in the next edition (DSM-V) due to be published in 2013. (Each edition of DSM introduces new categories as needed, and drops categories that are no longer needed.[xlvi])

I asked Neil, 'So what was she like?' He replied, 'She was quite ordinary, quite normal.' 'But surely,' I argued, 'the very fact that she stabbed her own children *must* mean she lacked empathy?' He said, 'Not really, because in psychiatry you can't judge a person's mind from their actions.' Here again, I had to politely disagree. To my mind, there are some actions that *by definition* reveal the mind behind them, and the cold-blooded murder of an innocent child is one of them. I'm not arguing that, once the action has been carried out, there is no need to interview or assess the person, as if their mind is transparent in the act. This is because at a minimum the law requires *mens rea* (the intent to commit the crime) as well as *actus reus* (the act itself). And there may be additional causes to ascertain (such as psychosis as a mitigating circumstance, or stress as an aggravating factor). But my argument is that, at the very least, a lack of empathy was transparent in her action. The exception might be the legal defence of 'automatism', where the individual was sleepwalking or acting without any awareness. So, assuming she was conscious, her act was unempathic.

Now that we've started exploring the question about the relationship between cruel acts and criminal responsibility, this naturally leads to a related question: should people with zero degrees of empathy be imprisoned if they commit a crime? This encompasses several different issues. First, the moral issue: if zero degrees of empathy is really a form of neurological disability, to what extent can such an individual who commits a crime be held responsible for what they have done? This gets tangled up with the free will debate, for, if zero degrees of empathy leaves an individual to some extent 'blind' to the impact of their actions on others' feelings, then surely they deserve our sympathy rather than punishment.

My own view is that sometimes the crime is so bad (e.g., murder) that imprisonment is necessary for three reasons: to protect society from the risk that this individual will repeat their crime; to signal society's disapproval of the crime; and to restore a sense of justice given the victim's feelings (or their family's feelings) that they were treated unjustly. I think all of these reasons for imprisonment can be justified. However, I have known individuals who have committed lesser crimes as a result of their zero degrees of empathy, for whom I would argue prison is *not* the right place.

Take Gary McKinnon, the young British man who hacked into the Pentagon from his bedroom in his parents' home in north London. When he appeared in our clinic with suspected Asperger Syndrome (which was confirmed), it became apparent that he had committed his crime *because* he was Zero-Positive. His strong drive to systemize enabled him to understand computers to a high level, and to become 'obsessed' with finding out what information the Pentagon kept on their computers and whether it was true. The fact that he did not attempt to hide his crime (since he left notes on each computer he hacked into saying that he had called) suggests he did not feel he was doing anything wrong, and also betrays his social naïveté. At the same time, his Zero-Positive status meant that at the time of his crime he was unable to imagine how the authorities would view his behaviour or what the social consequences could be for him.

When I interviewed him it was apparent that the risk of punishment was a sufficient deterrent such that I felt there was no risk of a repeat crime, and that his actions had not been motivated by any sense of malice. Nor had he hurt anyone or caused damage to anyone's property. The prospect of going to jail was terrifying for him, a socially isolated individual who suffered from clinical levels of depression and anxiety at the thought of life in prison. My view was that he posed no harm to society, and that as a society we might choose to treat a person with the neurological condition of Asperger Syndrome with dignity, not punishing them but showing them compassion and understanding, and offering them help. Going further, society might be better served by offering individuals like Gary a job, perhaps using his remarkable computer skills for the benefit of society, such as asking him to help the Pentagon and other institutions to improve their security systems.

A different case I was involved in was a man with suspected Asperger Syndrome who was being held in a secure prison in London for having followed a female stranger home from work and having touched her inappropriately. He was a forty-year-old man who had never had a girlfriend, still lived with his mother, and who didn't understand that what he had done was inappropriate. Nor did he have the first clue what the victim's feelings (of terror) would have been. Like Gary, he was suffering terribly in jail, not just because of his sensory hypersensitivity (the noise of a prison is deafening even to a typical individual) but also because of the social demands (being expected to share a prison cell with aggressive strangers and negotiate the verbal attacks from street-smart groups of prisoners in the canteen). To my mind, putting him in jail was like dropping a wheelchair-bound individual with physical disabilities into a swimming pool and expecting them to cope. It was the wrong environment for him despite the risk he could re-offend (he had zero understanding that what he had done was wrong). In a civilized, compassionate society we should be helping such individuals to find friendship, companionship and other forms of comfort, without jeopardizing anyone's safety. I am impressed with efforts to develop small, calm, compassionate but secure communities as alternatives to traditional prisons.

But let's return to the nature of human cruelty. Does replacing the word 'evil' with 'empathy erosion' really explain it? What are the alternative explanations? Leaving aside the religious concept of evil, which we have decided is not really a scientific explanation at all, the best-known alternative is political theorist Hannah Arendt's[322] analysis in terms of the 'banality of evil'. Arendt was an observer in the Jerusalem court case of Adolf Eichmann, one of the chief architects of the *Endlösung der Judenfrage* (the 'final solution to the Jewish question').[323] During the trial it became clear to Arendt that this man was neither mad nor different to the rest of us. He was quite *ordinary*. It was in this sense that she coined the phrase 'the banality of evil'.

The idea of the banality of evil also refers to *ordinary* factors that together can add up to an evil act. The concept stems from social psychological studies carried out by Solomon Asch,[xlvii] showing how 'conformity' can occur such that people can say one line is longer because everyone else is asserting this, even though the evidence before their eyes shows the opposite. In the same tradition, Stanley Milgram's[324] experiment showed 'obedience to authority', *ordinary* people being willing to inflict apparent electric shocks on others at levels that would kill them. Philip Zimbardo's Stanford Prison Experiment is also in this tradition, students being randomly assigned the roles of guard or prisoner in a simulated prison and who quickly started acting cruelly when in the role of guard.[325]

In addition, the phrase 'banality of evil' also relates to the fact that tens of thousands of *ordinary* individual Germans were complicit. Many of them could not be charged with war crimes later because they were just doing their job, just following orders, or just responsible for a tiny link in the chain. Eichmann and his fellow bureaucrats became immersed in the detail of their plans, such as timetabling the trains that transported Jews to the camps. They followed orders mechanically and without questioning them. Psychologist Christopher Browning's book *Ordinary Men* used Zimbardo's Stanford Prison experiment to explain the activities of the Reserve Police Battalion 101, a Nazi killing unit that murdered an estimated 40,000 Polish Jews in the Second World War. They were just following orders.[326]

Consider this simplification of the chain:

PERSON A: I simply had the list of Jews in my municipality. I did not round up the Jews but I did pass this list on when requested to do so.

PERSON B: I was told to go to these addresses, arrest these people and take them to the train station. That's all I did.

PERSON C: My job was to open the doors of the train – that was it.

PERSON D: My job was to direct the prisoners on to the train.

PERSON E: My job was to close the doors, not to ask where the train was going or why.

PERSON F: My job was simply to drive the train.

[Through all the other small links in the chain that led to . . .]

PERSON Z: My job was simply to turn on the showers out of which the poison gas was emitted.

None of these individuals may have had overall responsibility for the design or implementation of the big crime, only one small part of it. The banality of evil refers in part to how these small steps *together* bring about something awful, but each in isolation does not. Each is banal and does not warrant punishment. The banality of evil also refers to the fact that none of Persons A, B, C through to Z may have had zero degrees of empathy. They may be guilty of complicity but, having played their small part in the bigger sequence, may go home to their families or loved ones and express their empathy. The Nazi guard who shoots a prisoner in the daytime but then goes home at night, kisses his wife and reads a bedtime story to his young child seems to embody the contradiction. The reasons for any one individual's complicity may be varied. Some may simply be glad to have a job and be *afraid* to lose it if they don't follow their orders. Others may have an encapsulated *nationalist belief* that entitles them to treat non-nationals in a certain way. Whatever the individual reason for an individual contribution to the bigger sequence, these may be banal reasons.

The notion of the banality of evil has been challenged. David Cesarini[327] argued that Hannah Arendt only stayed for the beginning of the trial, when Eichmann wanted to appear as ordinary as possible. In fact, had she stayed longer, she would have seen how he exercised creativity in his murders; he was not just blindly following orders. In this sense, Eichmann's behaviour needs explaining not just in terms of social forces (important as these are) but individual factors (his reduced empathy) too.

One objection to the notion that cruelty is the result of low (affective) empathy is that it removes individual responsibility or free will (agency) from behaviour. (Notice that the banality of evil argument does the same, where individual responsibility is passed up the chain to someone higher up who is giving orders.) My own view is that the notion of free will and individual responsibility is an important concept to retain as we teach our children how to be and do good; and it is a useful concept guiding our own choices and actions. However, the notion of free will may be nothing more than a useful heuristic, and scientifically it seems hard to pin down. Most relevant, however agency or individual responsibility operates, a reduction in affective empathy will alter one's decision-making.

This is a good place to draw the strands together, to clarify the

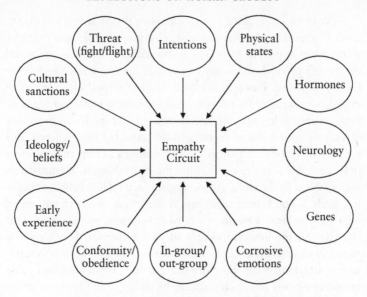

Figure 11: Empathy as Final Common Pathway

main claim in this book: that when acts of cruelty occur, it is because of the functioning of the empathy circuit. At several points I have called the empathy circuit the 'final common pathway' because a range of factors can impact and compromise its functioning. Figure 11 displays this central role clearly.

Let's briefly walk around the circle in Figure 11, through the 12 factors that can impact the empathy circuit. At the top are intentions, which some philosophers would argue are key to explaining acts of cruelty. I agree with this view, but the model highlights that an intention (to hurt someone) could not be acted upon if the empathy circuit was functioning normally. Our empathy would simply prevent the intention from being executed. Think of someone intending to hurt their dog and just as they move to strike him, their empathy circuit kicks in and stops them. Intentions can work in other ways too, including allowing you to switch off your empathy. Think of a surgeon whose intention to help means she has to cut the patient. She could only do this by reducing her empathy, allowing her to stick in the knife. In this example, intentions can also reduce one's empathy.

Next in the circle going anti-clockwise is threat. If you feel threatened, it is hard to also feel empathy. This may explain how empathy shuts down in people with Type B (borderlines) who can easily feel threatened given their history of insecure attachment, or even their history of abuse. Threat raises one's level of stress, which seems to impede any capacity for empathy. Next are social factors such as cultural sanctions. If your culture tells you it is acceptable to beat your servant or your horse or to burn those suspected of witchcraft, this too can also erode your empathy. This reminds us that cultural sanctions can play a key role in raising the general levels of empathy in society. Next in the circle are ideological factors, like beliefs or political goals. If you believe capitalism is the source of all evil you might be willing to leave a bomb in a crowded subway, switching off your empathy for the innocent victims of your terrorism. Another social factor is early experience, as we discussed in relation to how early secure attachment can promote the growth of empathy, and early insecure empathy can erode empathy by making it hard to trust others or making one feel threatened.

The next factor in the circle is conformity and obedience, both forces that were discussed in relation to Zimbardo's and Milgram's classic social psychological experiments, where our empathy may be reduced because of the institutional culture in which we find ourselves, or because of pressure from others. Equally important as a social factor are in-group/out-group identities. As social primates we show loyalty towards the group as a survival strategy, since we are weaker alone than in the protection of the group. This can have the effect of making us prioritize our own group's interests over those of the other group, leading us to show more compassion for our own group members than the other group. Empathy in this context is specific to a relationship which means the very same individual could be empathic to his or her own kin whilst being unempathic towards 'the enemy'.

The final psychological factors are corrosive emotions, like anger, hatred, jealousy or revenge. These have the power to reduce one's empathy, enabling acts of aggression.

Completing the factors in the circle are the biological factors such as genes, hormones, and neurological conditions, as we have discussed extensively. A final biological factor are physical states, such as tiredness, hunger, or drunkenness, all of which can erode empathy.

But at the centre of this circle of social, psychological, and biological factors is the empathy circuit. It reminds us how complex empathy is, that its functioning can be affected by at least these 12 factors.

We should be mindful that unempathic acts can have long-term consequences. Consider that, back in 1542, Martin Luther wrote a pamphlet entitled *Against the Jews* (calling on Christians to attack them); he advocated that synagogues should be burned and Jewish homes should be destroyed. *Four hundred years* later, the young Adolf Hitler quoted Martin Luther in *Mein Kampf* to give his own Nazi racist views some respectability, going on to create the concentration camps like the one nine-year-old Thomas Buergenthal was in, with gas chambers that ended up killing 6 million Jews. This shows how dangerous it can be if small unempathic acts go unnoticed. My cousin Sacha (who exposed contemporary anti-Semitism by posing as an anti-Semite himself, in the persona of his comic creation 'Borat') quotes Cambridge historian Ian Kershaw's chilling phrase: 'The path to Auschwitz was paved with indifference.'[xlviii]

But let's fast forward to human cruelty of the present day. If you ask most people for their clearest example of what they would call 'evil', they would point to the terrorist – a person who 'dispassionately' can kill innocent civilians to further his or her own political agenda. If my theory is correct, then we would have to say that terrorists have zero degrees of empathy. Is this true?

A twenty-six-year-old American hostage, Nick Berg, was videoed being beheaded by a man calling himself Abu Musab al-Zaquari, one of Osama bin Ladin's lieutenants in Iraq. The men in the video said the decapitation was revenge for the acts of torture being carried out by American forces in the Abu Ghraib prison west of Baghdad.[329] One might say that a terrorist who kills someone because they feel their land is under occupation is acting for very different reasons to a psychopath. Can we judge the same act (murder) as arising from the same switching off of the empathy circuit?

Our inclination might be to condemn a suicide bomber who comes over the border from Gaza into Jerusalem and blows up a café full of innocent teenagers, but, if we applied the same logic, we would have to also condemn Nelson Mandela when he was leader of Umkhonto we Sizwe, the armed wing of the African National Congress. He co-ordinated the bombing of military and government buildings, hoping that no one would get hurt but all the while recognizing that innocent people might get caught up in the blasts. Equally we would have to condemn Menachem Begin when he was leader of Irgun, a militant offshoot of the Haganah paramilitary organization that blew up the King David Hotel in Jerusalem on 22 July 1946, killing ninety-one people and injuring forty-six others, in an attempt to persuade the British to leave Palestine as part of the Zionist cause to create a Jewish homeland. Just as Mandela later became President of South Africa and winner of the Nobel Peace Prize, so Begin later became Prime Minister of Israel and joint winner of the Nobel Peace Prize with Egypt's President Anwar Sadat.

Because the target of the terrorist's unempathic act is selected because of the terrorist's belief (e.g., a belief that freedom and identity are being threatened), the act is not directly the result of an empathy deficit. The belief and/or the actual political context may be the driver of the behaviour. Nevertheless, at the moment of the act, one has to recognize that the terrorist's empathy is switched off – in flying a plane into the Twin Towers on 9/11, an individual (driven by a belief) no longer cared about the welfare and feelings of his victims. Tony Blair famously said when he gave the order to invade Iraq that 'history will forgive us',[330] but we cannot judge an act only by its distant outcomes, whilst ignoring its immediate outcomes. The act itself may be unempathic, irrespective of whether the ends justify the means.

There are of course degrees of violence. Murder may be an extreme case, and throwing a stone at someone may be a lesser case. This begs the question as to whether there are degrees of Zero-Negative? Clearly some forms of verbal abuse are not as hurtful as some forms of physical abuse. Shouting at or humiliating or offending someone can upset, frighten or anger them, but raping or physically attacking or torturing them can do all of these *and* injure or traumatize them, and can even be fatal. One would not want to say that a social faux pas is as bad as mugging someone. But can one really line up degrees of poor empathy? The Empathy Quotient (EQ) is one method that attempts to quantify how little or how much empathy a person has, but remains to be validated at the low end to see if it distinguishes these different forms of low empathy. Equally, at the level of neural activity in the empathy circuit, it would be interesting to compare the brains of those who commit mild but nevertheless inconsiderate unempathic acts (such as not bothering to flush the toilet for the next person) with those who commit more serious unempathic acts (like mugging people). My prediction would be that there would be degrees of under-activity in the empathy circuit, with the more serious forms showing even less activity in this circuit relative to the milder cases, but where both would be below the average for the general population.

I want to raise a deeper question about our human nature: namely, are we all capable of killing? According to the theory I have been developing in this book, it is only individuals who have low empathy that could attack or kill another person, that is, individuals whose empathy is temporarily or permanently shut down. Whether we are talking about 'premeditated' or an impulsive murder, the proposal is that such acts require a shutting off of empathy, either as a consequence of one's genes, early experience, or current state. This means that most people would not be capable of such cruel acts precisely because of their average or above average empathy levels. ('Current state' could include, for example, murder committed in the heat of an emotion, a 'crime of passion', a murder committed in self-defence, or in a 'blind rage' to protect a loved one. Equally it could include a crime committed during a transient psychotic illness.) Whatever the cause, the theory is that the very same empathy circuit must be affected.

Columbia University forensic psychiatrist Michael Stone formulated a twenty-two-point scale of evil to distinguish cases of Zero-Negative individuals who end up in jail for murder. It is an attempt at a classification of types of murder/violent crime, but reads as more of a list of the causes of murder and violence (including situational causes); they are unlikely to correspond to twenty-two meaningful distinctions within the brain. (For those who are interested in the details, Stone's levels (summarized) are in the notes.[xlix])

But back to the key question behind this book. Does Zero-Negative explain human cruelty? To answer this question we need to look at actual cases of cruelty and ask, despite their surface differences, could they all arise from the same underlying neural empathy circuit being under-active? Not all the data are yet in to answer this question, but the claim is exactly this. In Chapter 1 we surveyed many types of 'evil' acts. We can assume that whatever the nature of the act (be it physical unempathic acts – physical violence, murder, torture, rape, committing genocide, etc. – or non-physical unempathic acts – deception, mockery, verbal abuse, etc.), at the very moment of the act, the empathy circuit 'goes down'. In an otherwise normal individual, this may be a transient turning off of the system. In someone who is Type B, P or N, their empathy system may be permanently down.

This raises the question as to how the empathy circuit could be switched off irreversibly, or at least in a long-term fashion. We saw in Chapter 3 how a range of early environmental factors (e.g., emotional abuse and neglect) can deplete our 'internal pot of gold', our sense of self-worth and ability to trust people or form secure attachments to others. Equally, in Chapter 5 we saw how a range of genes can affect empathy, presumably by affecting the empathy circuit. Some of these genetic and environmental factors also affect molecular pathways such as the sex steroid hormonal system, with the result of having permanent, *organizational* effects on brain development.

The concept of 'organizational' effects in neuroscience echoes the concept of 'critical' or 'sensitive' periods in developmental psychology.[1] We saw that the prenatal sex steroid hormones (including testosterone) have effects on the developing brain that appear irreversible. The higher one's prenatal testosterone, the more the brain is 'masculinized' towards stronger systemizing and weaker empathy.[295, 331]

So, back to the range of 'evil' acts: are they all the result of such early environmental (emotional deprivation) or biological factors (genes and/or hormones, neurotransmitters, etc.) affecting the empathy circuit? Josef Fritzl, you recall, repeatedly raped his daughter Elisabeth, whom he had imprisoned for twenty-four years. After listening to ten hours of videotaped evidence from her at his trial, he said, 'I realized for the first time how cruel I was to Elisabeth.' Clearly this was a man in whom empathy does not come naturally, since he began to figure it out only when another person's pain – his own daughter's, no less – was rammed down his throat. Psychiatrist Adelheid Kastner gave evidence at the trial and said that in her opinion Fritzl had been 'born to rape', implying some innate factor. It may be that in the future, such cases of Zero-Negative will be genetically tested so that we can understand which of the suite of genes contributes to such extremes of low empathy. Equally Kastner attested that Fritzl's behaviour was rooted in his childhood, since he had been repeatedly beaten by his mother.[332]

Eric Harris and Dylan Klebold carried out the notorious killings of their classmates and teachers at Columbine High School in 1999. Their homemade bombs were badly wired but were intended to kill six hundred people in the cafeteria. Consistent with the Zero-Negative theory, Klebold was a depressive, suicidal character (which is at least compatible with him being Type B), while Harris was a classic psychopath (Type P), a diagnosis confirmed by psychologist Robert Hare. Harris wrote in his journal:

> Isn't America supposed to be the land of the free? How come, if I'm free, I can't deprive a stupid fucking dumbshit of his possessions if he leaves them sitting on the front seat of his fucking van out in plain sight and in the middle of fucking nowhere on a Frifuckingday night? Natural selection. Fucker should be shot.[333]

Sadly there is no end to such examples of zero degrees of empathy and while we cannot test the theory in each individual case, the early development and/or psychological profiles of those who commit such crimes frequently if not invariably involve such risk factors.

My next question concerns whether, if empathy is missing in childhood or adolescence, can it develop later? Melissa Todorovic is in a Toronto prison for being the 'puppeteer' behind a murder.[334] Aged fifteen, she persuaded her seventeen-year-old boyfriend (known as D. B., and who has mild learning difficulties) to stab a girl called Stefanie Rengel, whom she had never met but of whom she was jealous. After months of nagging him and threatening to withhold sexual favours, shockingly the boy agreed to her request. He lured Stefanie out of her parents' house and stabbed her six times.[335] He told Melissa what he had done, and she then phoned Stefanie's phone to check she was really dead. Having confirmed he had done what she ordered, she then agreed to have sex with him. Stefanie died, and the courts ruled that Melissa was as guilty as her boyfriend in having had the *mens rea* (the intention to commit the act) even if she did not commit the actual act. She was deemed to be guilty of conspiracy. Two years on, she still feels no remorse. Psychologists and psychiatrists examining her case argue that the adolescent brain is still developing as late as the age of twenty-five[336] and that we should therefore keep an open mind to the possibility that she is simply suffering an extreme developmental delay in her empathy.

As we saw in Chapter 3, such examples of Conduct Disorder strongly predict Type P (Psychopathic Personality Disorder). The fact that this is not seen in 100 per cent of cases means that a subgroup of those who commit extreme crimes of this kind do eventually develop sufficient self-control and/or emotion-regulation and/or moral awareness to change their path onto a more empathic one. I suspect this subgroup is rare.

The issue of prison sentencing may of course ignore the scientific evidence, and instead focus on the feelings of the victim's family. Sitting around the Friday night dinner table in Toronto we discussed Melissa Todorovic's case: how should society react? Every opinion was represented at the table. At one extreme was Lynn's view: 'If she's taken a life, then she loses the right to her own life. A life sentence should mean just that. Throw away the key and let her rot in jail!'

At the other extreme was Avi's view: even those who commit 'evil' crimes should be given a chance to recognize their 'mistakes' and learn from them: 'Peter Sutcliffe [the Yorkshire Ripper, who killed thirteen women, many of them working as prostitutes[li]] has been in prison for almost thirty years. He should be allowed to enjoy some years of freedom – he's paid a fair price.'

I certainly situate myself closer to this end of the spectrum of opinion. I remember sitting in the Beth Shalom synagogue in Cambridge on the night of Kol Nidre. Peter Lipton, a friend and an atheist philosopher, was giving the sermon on the theme of 'atonement':

> If we treat another person as essentially bad, we dehumanize him or her. If we take the view that every human being has some good in them, even if it is only 0.1 per cent of their make-up, then by focusing on their good part, we humanize them. By acknowledging and attending to and rewarding their good part, we allow it to grow, like a small flower in a desert.

I found it a provocative idea because the implication of this attitude is that no one – however evil we paint them to be – should be treated as 100 per cent bad, or as beyond responding to a humane approach. The question is whether one can push this to its logical conclusion: if unambiguously 'evil' individuals (a candidate for this category might be Hitler) felt remorse for their crimes, and had been punished, would we try to focus on their good qualities, with a view to rehabilitating them? My own view is that we should do this – no matter how bad their crime. It is the only way we can establish that we are showing empathy to the perpetrator, not just repeating the crime of turning the perpetrator into an object, and thus dehumanizing them. To do that renders us no better than the person we punish.

Interestingly, as I write this, Ronnie Lee Gardner (a convicted murderer) was executed by a firing squad in the state of Utah. By all accounts, he had faced up to his own guilt and had spent his adult life trying to help prevent other young people experiencing similar neglect and abuse that he had experienced and which had contributed to his crimes. But, despite this apparent change in him as he grew older, the state of Utah judiciary felt he had to be killed. What interests me is – even in modern America – it is possible to find five police officers who will volunteer for the task of executioner, to shoot an unarmed prisoner tied to a chair. Even more striking to me was that a doctor placed a disc above Ronnie's heart to serve as a target for the executioners. Did this doctor think he was doing his job as a doctor? Where was the empathy in the judge who convicted Ronnie to die, or in the executioners who pulled the trigger? His niece wept at his death, seeing him as a person who was loved.

As you can tell, I am against the death sentence. It is not just barbaric (and ironically makes the State as unempathic as the person they seek to punish), but it closes down the possibility of change or development within the individual. We know there is already evidence that components of empathy (such as emotion recognition) can be learned.[316, 337, 338] These methods only scratch the surface in terms of what could be tried, and we need to remain open-minded that other aspects of empathy – beyond emotion-recognition – can be taught and learned. Counselling and other psychological therapies such as role-playing techniques purport to be aiming to encourage empathy, and it would be valuable to have systematic studies to show if these are working. The extent to which these can work for people at different points on the empathy curve also needs to be tested. For example, it would not be surprising if someone who is slightly below average in their EQ slightly boosted their empathy following intervention. Whether someone who is truly at zero degrees of empathy can be helped to acquire it, and, if so, whether it can ever reach 'normal' levels, remains to be established.

SUPER-EMPATHY?

In Chapter 2 we saw how empathy is 'distributed' along a normal bell curve. Up until now we have considered the zero extreme and hardly touched on the other extreme of empathy, those with super-levels. What are these people like? Zurich neuroscientist Tania Singer gave a presentation on this topic in a beautiful conference centre in Erice in Sicily. She had scanned the brain of a Buddhist monk who had spent his adult life learning to control both his reaction to his own pain and to that of others. He could remain calm and at peace when he was sitting for long periods of time in uncomfortable positions, he could control his heart rate via meditation, and he could show empathy towards any living person or animal. Tania demonstrated that the monk's brain was in a state of hyper-activity in the empathy circuit, when viewing other people's facial expressions.

At the end of her fascinating lecture, I asked her whether we really could conclude that the monk's behaviour comprised super-empathy. She elegantly argued that if the monk was suppressing the self-aspects of the pain matrix in the brain (and the brain scans suggested this was the case), then perhaps the over-activity in his empathy circuit could indicate that he could tune in exclusively to the other person's emotional state, setting aside his own. On the face of it, this is an excellent demonstration of the suppression of the mirror neuron system and of superior empathy.

But I remain unconvinced by this interpretation. First, if someone can suppress their own pain sensations, while that might be a useful skill on the battlefield or in competitive sports, it is not clear that this is required for super-empathy. Secondly, if you suppress your *appropriate* emotional response to another person's pain, how is that empathic? Whatever the monk was doing, and it was clearly abnormal, it doesn't fit my definition of empathy. If you go through a series of changing emotions, from pleasure to pain, and a Buddhist monk smiles calmly at you as your emotions change, as if to say 'I accept you non-judgementally', I think this would feel out of tune with your feelings. At the very least, if you were in pain, then an expression of sympathy might be nice to see and feel, to show that he cared. The *detachment* of the normal empathic response to my mind disqualifies the monk from being a candidate for a super-empathizer.

Some people have tried to convince me that super-empathy would be an unpleasant state to be in because one would be in a permanent state of distress at anyone else's distress in the vicinity or even via hearsay. It could be both overwhelming and depressing to be emotionally responding to such a lot of sadness, especially if the mirror neuron system induces a similar emotion in oneself to that being expressed by another person. I think this is an intriguing notion, that super-empathy might itself be maladaptive, but again I remain sceptical since, if an individual is overwhelmed to the point of not being able to separate their own emotions from someone else's, in what sense can they be said to have super-empathy? In such a state of confusion, they may simply be distressed rather than empathic.

Having spent some time discussing what I think super-empathy is not, it behoves me to say what I think super-empathy might be. Recall Hannah, in Chapter 2, the psychotherapist who rapidly tuned into anyone's feelings and who verbalized their feelings with sensitivity but with great accuracy. To my mind, she is a good candidate for someone whose Empathizing Mechanism is tuned at Level 6. A second candidate for someone with super-empathy is Archbishop Desmond Tutu. In a recent documentary[339] discussing his remarkable role in the anti-Apartheid struggle, as he sat in the Truth and Reconciliation Hearings listening to black victims telling their personal stories to the white police officers and prison guards who had tortured or killed their loved ones, Tutu had to visibly bite his own hand to stop himself crying out loud, so strong was the desire to express the pain and distress he felt at hearing of another person's suffering. But, as he explained in the interview, these hearings were to acknowledge the victims' emotions, not his. To have openly wept would have been to make his own emotions the focus of attention, and to take away attention from those of the victim. For this reason, he stifled his deep upset as best he could.

Recognizing that the white guards and officers too needed the opportunity to experience forgiveness was partly motivated by his deep religious sense, but it was also a recognition that even the aggressor was a person who deserved dignity, and the opportunity to show remorse. But he acknowledged that remorse was not always possible. He recalled how the then Minister of Justice, James Kruger, said of the death of black activist Steve Biko that 'his death left me cold'.[340] Tutu asks, as we have in this book, what has happened to a man that he feels nothing at the death of another human being?

Figure 12: Desmond Tutu, who chaired the Truth and Reconciliation Hearings and played a key role in toppling the racist Apartheid South African regime

As far as I know, the brains of individuals like Hannah or like Desmond Tutu have never been scanned but we can make a clear prediction: that they would show over-activity of the very same empathy circuit that is under-active in those who are Zero-Negative.

Clearly, being Zero-Negative is not a good state. My speculation about the opposite extreme, super-empathy, is that this is wholly positive, but this may be true only from a very altruistic perspective. Altruism, however, is not necessarily a sustainable lifestyle 24/7. If you focus only on others, there is a risk that you neglect your own needs. Too much of a focus on your own needs could result in a self-centredness which itself carries dangers of becoming isolated from social support. Presumably the reason that empathy is a bell curve (with the majority of people showing moderate rather than high levels of empathy) is because moderate empathy levels are most adaptive. Being too other-centred means one would never pursue one's own ambitions, or act competitively, for fear of upsetting or diminishing others. Being too self-centred has the advantage of pursuing one's own ambitions to the exclusion of all else, where the pay-off may be considerable (especially in the world of business or in the accumulation of resources), but, while the 'ruthless bastard' may become richer or more powerful, he or she also makes more enemies in the process. Striking the balance at majority levels of empathy may be an evolved adaptation that confers on the individual the benefits of empathy without its disadvantages.

I would be horrified if readers of this book took from it the conclusion that empathy was better than logic, since I hope I have argued convincingly that both have their value. In the case of Zero-Positive, we see the value of logic (strong systemizing) in stark relief. And, when it comes to problem solving, clearly many situations require both logic and empathy. They are not mutually exclusive. Whether the conflict is domestic, or in the work place, or in international relations, the combination of logic and empathy has a lot to recommend it. This somewhat obvious claim nevertheless needs to be made simply because of the neglect of empathy in many scenarios.

My definition of reduced empathy (in Chapter 1) was when we cease to treat a person as a person, with their own feelings, and start to treat them as an object. But it could be reasonably asked: don't we all do this all the time to each other? We enjoy a friendship because the person gives us something; we enjoy a sexual relationship because the person's body is an object; we employ a person because they provide a service we need; and we might enjoy watching someone for their beauty or athletic grace. These all involve aspects of the person as an object.

My reply to this would be that if our empathy is turned on, then, all the while we are treating the person as an object, we are simultaneously aware of or sensitive to their feelings. If their emotional state changed, such that they were suddenly upset, we would not just continue with our current activity, but we would check what was wrong and what they might need. If the friendship is based purely on what we gain from the relationship, such that we abandon the person when they are unable to still provide that, it would be not just a shallow relationship, but an unempathic one. But I should qualify the definition of empathy by adding that the point at which we objectify another person while simultaneously switching off our sensitivity to their emotions is the *starting point* towards zero degrees of empathy. It is not the end-point, since, as we have seen in the catalogue of crimes that people commit, such a state of mind simply makes it possible to behave in more and more hurtful ways.

EMPATHY AS AN UNDER-UTILIZED RESOURCE

One of my motivations for writing this book was to persuade you that empathy is *one of the most valuable resources in our world*. Erosion of empathy is an important global issue related to the health of our communities, be they small (like families) or big (like nations). Families can be torn apart by brothers who can no longer talk to each other, or couples who have developed an awful mistrust of each other, or a child and parent who misunderstand each other's intentions. Without empathy we risk the breakdown of relationships, we become capable of hurting others, and we can cause conflict. With empathy we have a resource to resolve conflict, increase community cohesion, and dissolve another person's pain.

I think we have taken empathy for granted, and thus to some extent overlooked it. Psychology as a science virtually ignored it for a century. Educators focusing on literacy and mathematics have also largely ignored it. We just assume empathy will develop in every child, come what may. We put little time, effort or money into nurturing it. Our politicians almost never mention it, despite the fact that they need it more than anyone. This book follows on the heels of Jeremy Rifkin's historical account *The Empathic Civilization* and Frans de Waal's evolutionary account *The Age of Empathy* in putting empathy back on the agenda.[liii] But, until recently, neuroscientists hardly questioned what empathy is. I hope that by now you realize what a powerful resource we as a species have, at our very fingertips, if only we prioritize it.

In case this talk about the power of empathy seems to lack real-world implications, let's bring it down to earth by considering the breakdown of a relationship between two nations: the Middle-East conflict, which raged through most of the twentieth century and continues with no sign of abating. If only each community could see the other's point of view, and empathize.

The early Zionists in part were Jewish refugees of waves of anti-Semitism, many of whose families had been persecuted in the Russian pogroms of the nineteenth century and under Nazism in the twentieth. My grandfather, Michael Greenblatt, was one such early Zionist, who fled Lithuanian pogroms at the age of six, arriving by boat into the city of Montreal in 1906. Whenever I visited him he was busy fund-raising to help the creation of the new homeland of Israel. He became active in the exciting project of building a world-class Hebrew University, on Mount Scopus in Jerusalem. Israel has enjoyed remarkable successes, creating cities with world-class hospitals, orchestras and research centres – but from the outset became embroiled in a tragic string of military conflicts. Remarkably, just one day after the State of Israel was founded in 1948, it was invaded by its Arab neighbours. Why?

In part it may be because many Palestinians understandably felt displaced by the creation of the State of Israel, a consequence that was perhaps underestimated by the United Nations which authorized the new state. Whatever the original cause, the consequence has been sixty years of Palestinian bombers and Israeli tanks in a cycle of tit-for-tat attacks, leading to ever more human suffering. By this point in the cycle, many on both sides see only their own point of view and – in this sense – have lost their empathy for the other. It is clear that military solutions have not worked, and I argue that *the only way forward will be through empathy*. Fortunately, there is evidence that those in the Middle East have not lost their empathy in any permanent or enduring way. I sat in Alyth Gardens synagogue in Golders Green in north London last year. Two men went up on the stage.

The first one spoke: 'I am Ahmed, and I am a Palestinian. My son died in the Intifada, killed by an Israeli bullet. I come to wish you all Shabbat Shalom.'

Then the other man spoke: 'I am Moishe, and I am an Israeli. My son also died in the Intifada, killed by a homemade petrol bomb thrown by a Palestinian teenager. I come to wish you all Salaam Alaikem.'

I was shocked: here were two fathers, from different sides of the political divide, united by their grief and now embracing each other's language. How had they met? Moishe had taken up the opportunity offered by a charity called The Parents Circle[liii] for Israelis and Palestinians to make free phone calls directly into each others' homes, to express their empathy to bereaved parents on the other side of the barbed wire fence. Ahmed described how he had been at home in Gaza one day when the phone rang. It was Moishe, at that time a stranger in Jerusalem, who had taken that brave first step. They both openly wept down the phone. Neither had ever met or even spoken to someone from the other community, but both told the other they knew what the other was going through.

Moishe told Ahmed: 'We are the same: we have both lost our son. Your pain is my pain.' Ahmed had replied, 'This suffering must end before there are more fathers like you and me who come to know the awful pain of losing a beloved son.'

The two fathers now tour mosques and synagogues internationally, raising awareness of the need for empathy and fundraising for the charity. Of course, this is just a tiny step, but each drop of empathy waters the flower of peace.[liv]

Empathy is like a universal solvent.[lv] Any problem immersed in empathy becomes soluble. It is effective as a way of anticipating and resolving interpersonal problems, whether this is a marital conflict, an international conflict, a problem at work, difficulties in a friendship, political deadlocks, a family dispute, or a problem with the neighbour. I hope you have been persuaded that this resource is a better way to resolve problems than the alternatives (such as guns, laws, or religion). And, unlike the arms industry that costs trillions of dollars to maintain, or the prison service and legal system that cost millions of dollars to keep oiled, empathy is free. And, unlike religion, empathy cannot, by definition, oppress anyone.

Appendix 1:
The Empathy Quotient (EQ)

THE EMPATHY QUOTIENT (EQ) – ADULT VERSION

How to fill out the questionnaire *Below are a list of statements. Please read each statement very carefully and rate how strongly you agree or disagree with it. There are no right or wrong answers, or trick questions.*

	Strongly Agree	Slightly Agree	Slightly Disagree	Strongly Disagree
1. I can easily tell if someone else wants to enter a conversation.				
2. I find it difficult to explain to others things that I understand easily, when they don't understand it first time.				
3. I really enjoy caring for other people.				
4. I find it hard to know what to do in a social situation.				
5. People often tell me that I went too far in driving my point home in a discussion.				

	Strongly Agree	Slightly Agree	Slightly Disagree	Strongly Disagree
6. It doesn't bother me too much if I am late meeting a friend.				
7. Friendships and relationships are just too difficult, so I tend not to bother with them.				
8. I often find it difficult to judge if something is rude or polite.				
9. In a conversation, I tend to focus on my own thoughts rather than on what my listener might be thinking.				
10. When I was a child, I enjoyed cutting up worms to see what would happen.				
11. I can pick up quickly if someone says one thing but means another.				
12. It is hard for me to see why some things upset people so much.				
13. I find it easy to put myself in somebody else's shoes.				
14. I am good at predicting how someone will feel.				

	Strongly Agree	Slightly Agree	Slightly Disagree	Strongly Disagree
15. I am quick to spot when someone in a group is feeling awkward or uncomfortable.				
16. If I say something that someone else is offended by, I think that that's their problem, not mine.				
17. If anyone asked me if I liked their haircut, I would reply truthfully, even if I didn't like it.				
18. I can't always see why someone should have felt offended by a remark.				
19. Seeing people cry doesn't really upset me.				
20. I am very blunt, which some people take to be rudeness, even though this is unintentional.				
21. I don't tend to find social situations confusing.				
22. Other people tell me I am good at understanding how they are feeling and what they are thinking.				

	Strongly Agree	Slightly Agree	Slightly Disagree	Strongly Disagree
23. When I talk to people, I tend to talk about their experiences rather than my own.				
24. It upsets me to see an animal in pain.				
25. I am able to make decisions without being influenced by people's feelings.				
26. I can easily tell if someone else is interested or bored with what I am saying.				
27. I get upset if I see people suffering on news programmes.				
28. Friends usually talk to me about their problems as they say that I am very understanding.				
29. I can sense if I am intruding, even if the other person doesn't tell me.				
30. People sometimes tell me that I have gone too far with teasing.				

	Strongly Agree	Slightly Agree	Slightly Disagree	Strongly Disagree
31. Other people often say that I am insensitive, though I don't always see why.				
32. If I see a stranger in a group, I think that it is up to them to make an effort to join in.				
33. I usually stay emotionally detached when watching a film.				
34. I can tune into how someone else feels rapidly and intuitively.				
35. I can easily work out what another person might want to talk about.				
36. I can tell if someone is masking their true emotion.				
37. I don't consciously work out the rules of social situations.				
38. I am good at predicting what someone will do.				
39. I tend to get emotionally involved with a friend's problems.				

	Strongly Agree	Slightly Agree	Slightly Disagree	Strongly Disagree
40. I can usually appreciate the other person's viewpoint, even if I don't agree with it.				

© SBC/SJW Feb 1998

How to Score Your EQ

Score two points for each of the following items if you answered 'strongly agree' or one point if you answered 'slightly agree': 1, 3, 11, 13, 14, 15, 21, 22, 24, 26, 27, 28, 29, 34, 35, 36, 37, 38, 39, 40.

Score two points for each of the following items if you answered 'definitely disagree' or one point if you answered 'slightly disagree': 2, 4, 5, 6, 7, 8, 9, 10, 12, 16, 17, 18, 19, 20, 23, 25, 30, 31, 32, 33.

Simply add up all the points you have scored to obtain your total EQ score.

How to Interpret Your EQ Score

- *0–32 = **low** (most people with Asperger Syndrome or high-functioning autism score about 20)*
- *33–52 = **average range** (most women score about 47 and most men score about 42)*
- *52–63 is **above average***
- *64–80 is **very high***
- *80 = **maximum***

Details on the norms, validity, reliability and other statistical issues relating to the tests shown in these Appendices are given in the original articles published in the scientific journals, cited earlier.

THE EMPATHY QUOTIENT (CHILD VERSION)[lvi]

Please complete by ticking the appropriate box for each statement

	Definitely Agree	Slightly Agree	Slightly Disagree	Definitely Disagree
1. My child likes to look after other people.				
2. My child often doesn't understand why some things upset other people so much.				
3. My child would not cry or get upset if a character in a film died.				
4. My child is quick to notice when people are joking.				
5. My child enjoys cutting up worms, or pulling the legs off insects.				
6. My child has stolen something they wanted from their sibling or friend.				
7. My child has trouble forming friendships.				

	Definitely Agree	Slightly Agree	Slightly Disagree	Definitely Disagree
8. When playing with other children, my child spontaneously takes turns and shares toys.				
9. My child can be blunt giving their opinions, even when these may upset someone.				
10. My child would enjoy looking after a pet.				
11. My child is often rude or impolite without realizing it.				
12. My child has been in trouble for physical bullying.				
13. At school, when my child understands something they can easily explain it clearly to others.				
14. My child has one or two close friends, as well as several other friends.				

	Definitely Agree	Slightly Agree	Slightly Disagree	Definitely Disagree
15. My child listens to others' opinions, even when different from their own.				
16. My child shows concern when others are upset.				
17. My child can seem so preoccupied with their own thoughts that they don't notice others getting bored.				
18. My child blames other children for things that they themselves have done.				
19. My child gets very upset if they see an animal in pain.				
20. My child sometimes pushes or pinches someone if they are annoying them.				
21. My child can easily tell when another person wants to enter into conversation with them.				

	Definitely Agree	Slightly Agree	Slightly Disagree	Definitely Disagree
22. My child is good at negotiating for what they want.				
23. My child would worry about how another child would feel if they weren't invited to a party.				
24. My child gets upset at seeing others crying or in pain.				
25. My child likes to help new children integrate in class.				
26. My child has been in trouble for name-calling or teasing.				
27. My child tends to resort to physical aggression to get what they want.				

How to Score Your Child's EQ

Score two points for each of the following items if you answered 'strongly agree' or one point if you answered 'slightly agree': 1, 4, 8, 10, 13, 14, 15, 16, 19, 21, 22, 23, 24, 25.

Score two points for each of the following items if you answered 'definitely disagree' or one point if you answered 'slightly disagree': 2, 3, 5, 6, 7, 9, 11, 12, 17, 18, 20, 26, 27.

Simply add up all the points you have scored to obtain your total EQ score.

How to Interpret Your EQ Score

- *0–24 = **low** (most children with Asperger Syndrome or High-functioning autism score about 14)*
- *25–44 = **average range** (most girls score about 40 and most boys score about 34)*
- *45–49 is **above average***
- *50–54 is **very high***
- *54 = **maximum***

Details on the norms, validity, reliability and other statistical issues relating to the tests shown in these Appendices are given in the original articles published in the scientific journals, cited earlier.

Appendix 2: How to Spot Zero Degrees of Empathy (Negative)

HOW TO SPOT BORDERLINES

A psychiatrist or clinical psychologist examining someone with suspected Borderline Personality Disorder turns to DSM-IV (the *Diagnostic and Statistical Manual*, 4th edn.), the book of rules on their desk for how to diagnose a mental health condition. This states that the person needs to show at least five out of eight of the following signs:

(1) *Unstable and intense interpersonal relationships*:
  - fluctuating from clingy dependency to withdrawal, from being super-nice to unreasonably demanding, from seeing someone as all good (idealization) to all bad (devaluation)
  - endlessly searching for the perfect caregiver
  - wanting to be soul-mates and yet fearing intimacy, believing they will lose their identity and cease to exist
  - highly manipulative in relationships (e.g., hypochondriacs, inappropriately seductive, making suicidal threats) to get attention.

(2) *Impulsivity*:
  - potentially self-destructive drug or alcohol abuse
  - sexual promiscuity, stealing, excessive spending
  - extreme eating or extreme dieting.

(3) *Extreme mood swings*:
  - from depression to anger to elation and enthusiasm
  - each mood only lasts a few hours.

(4) *Inability to control anger*:
  - expressed as outbursts of rage and getting into fights
  - throwing objects at people during domestic arguments

- threatening them with knives, often triggered by something trivial
- anger is directed towards their closest relationships, such as a child, parent, therapist or partner.

(5) *Suicidal threats or self-mutilation*:
- a way of saying 'I am in pain, please help me!'
- suicidal threats are eventually ignored by others as they realize these are attention-seeking.

(6) *Identity confusion*:
- unsure about their self-image, career, values, friends, or even their sexual orientation
- feeling that they are faking it and will be discovered as a fake
- easy prey to a cult leader offering to tell them who they are and how to think.

(7) *Extreme emptiness*:
- an inner loneliness or boredom
- the mood swings and drug abuse can be an attempt to escape the inner emptiness.

(8) *Extreme fear of abandonment*:
- clinging to others
- being terrified of being alone, in case they cease to exist.

HOW TO SPOT SOMEONE WITH ANTI-SOCIAL PERSONALITY DISORDER

Diagnosed when someone shows a pervasive pattern of disregard for and violation of others occurring since age 15 years, as indicated by three (or more) of the following:

(1) *Failure to conform to social norms of lawfulness*:
- performing acts that are arrestable offences.

(2) *Deceitfulness*:
- repeated lying
- use of aliases
- conning people for personal profit or pleasure.

(3) *Impulsivity or failure to plan ahead*

(4) *Irritability and aggression*[lvii]
- physical fights and assaults.

(5) *Reckless disregard for the safety of oneself or others*

(6) *Consistent irresponsibility:*
- repeated failure to sustain work commitments
- repeated failure to honour financial obligations.

(7) *Lack of remorse:*
- indifference to having hurt, mistreated, or stolen from someone
- rationalizing having hurt, mistreated, or stolen from someone.

HOW TO SPOT A YOUNG PERSON WITH CONDUCT DISORDER

Persistently violating the basic rights of others or societal norms, manifested by three (or more) of the following in the past 12 months:

(1) *Aggression to people and animals:*
- bullying people, threatening, or intimidating others
- initiating physical fights
- using a weapon that can cause serious physical harm (e.g., a bat, brick, broken bottle, knife, gun)
- being physically cruel to people and/or animals
- stealing while confronting a victim (e.g., mugging, purse snatching, extortion, armed robbery)
- forcing someone to have sex.

(2) *Destruction of property:*
- deliberately engaging in fire setting with the intention of causing serious damage
- deliberately destroying others' property.

(3) *Deceitfulness or theft:*
- breaking into someone else's house, building, or car
- lying to obtain goods or favours or to avoid obligations (i.e., 'cons' others)
- stealing (e.g., shoplifting, forgery).

(4) *Serious violations of rules:*
- staying out at night despite parental prohibitions, before the age of thirteen

- running away from home overnight
- truanting from school, beginning before the age of thirteen.

HOW TO RECOGNIZE A NARCISSIST

People who are Zero-Negative Type N show five (or more) of the following:

- a grandiose sense of self-importance
- a preoccupation with fantasies of success and power, beauty, or ideal love
- a belief that he or she is 'special' and should associate with people who are also of high status
- a need for excessive admiration
- a sense of entitlement
- a style of exploiting others
- unempathic
- envy of others or a belief others are envious of him or her
- arrogant attitudes.

Notes

i Her name has been anonymized as I have not been able to trace her to seek her consent for her real name to be used.

ii The professor regretted that the data had been collected in such inhumane conditions but felt it was still worth presenting in his lecture some forty years later, since much had been learned from it. I was personally repulsed by this use of data – even for medical teaching – feeling that the ends did not justify the means. Unethical science is unethical science.

iii Thomas grew up to be a founder of UNICEF and is now a judge in The Hague, where he has spent more than forty years working in human rights.

iv Sounds paradoxical, doesn't it? To make this more concrete, if while organizing a project you turn to your child who is feeling upset and say 'I can't talk to you now – I'm late for work', at that very moment you have switched off your empathy.

v Esther's husband was also hacked to death by the machete-wielding child rebels. Fifty-six people were killed on that July night, and many more injured.

vi *Guardian*, 5 December 2008: 'Age 1–90: the victims of hidden war against women', by Diane Taylor.

vii My colleague Alan Leslie, now a professor at Rutgers University, developed a fascinating theory when I worked with him in London in the 1980s. It was called 'meta-representation', which provides a nice mechanism for this 'double-mindedness' because it involves your own (primary) representation of the world and a representation of someone else's representation of the world. See also Leslie, A., Pretence and representation: the origins of 'theory of mind'. *Psychological Review* 94, 412–26 (1987).

viii Let's split hairs for a second (always a favourite party game). Supposing I see you struggle with the suitcase and I experience a pang of sympathy, but turn away. I would say that I have still empathized. Acting on an empathic response is I think a third stage (beyond recognition and response) that I don't think is an intrinsic part of empathy. The *desire* to help alleviate a person's suffering should I think be part of empathy, but whether you actually do anything about it is subject to a hundred and one different factors. (Do you have the means to help? Are you physically close enough to help? Can you stop doing what you are currently doing? Do you believe that someone else will intervene instead? And so on.) So, provided you have experienced the appropriate emotion (e.g., 'I sympathize with your predicament and wish I could help'), to me, that's enough to say that you empathized. If on the other hand you only half-experienced the appropriate emotion (e.g., 'I sympathize with your predicament but I don't really care what happens to you'), to me, that's not enough to count as empathy. The emotional response phase of empathy has to be the full-blown thing, the full monty. Half-hearted empathy is not really empathy at all.

ix The main measure of empathy is called the Interpersonal Reactivity Index,[11] and it is widely used. The problem is that, while it produces a nice normal distribution, it is a questionnaire that measures more than just empathy. For example, it contains questions about how easily you fantasize and – while interesting – this is not directly relevant to empathy.

x I have divided the empathy bell curve into seven levels, but this is somewhat arbitrary because all of our research to date suggests it is truly a continuum, a seamless dimension. But these seven levels are nevertheless useful because they help to bring out some qualitative differences that arise as you surf the empathy bell curve, differences which may be less apparent if a purely incremental, quantitative approach is taken.

xi Barbara Oakley has edited an interesting book on *Pathological Altruism* (Oxford, 2011), a state in which people are so moved by others' emotions that they are overwhelmed by them. I don't see that those at Level 6 (super-empathy) necessarily have to suffer from the amount they empathize, though this may be relevant to a subgroup. Those at Level 6 warrant more study in their own right.

xii Mike Lombardo correctly points out that these two functions of the vMPFC do not involve the very same area: coding the emotional valence is slightly further back in the brain, whereas the self-awareness function is slightly more towards the front of the brain.[26] See also Damasio's excellent book *Descarte's Error* (New York, 1994).

xiii There is a debate about whether he lost his empathy or lost the ability for 'self-regulation'. To me these are very much entwined. Patients with lesions in this area have difficulty in using their own emotions to guide appropriate social behaviour, and this type of process is one that is critical in responding to another's emotion with the appropriate emotion.[29–31]

xiv A later CT scan suggests Phineas's brain damage was more on the left side. His case is consistent with damage to a part of his empathy circuit, although from such a historic case it is hard to know if he only suffered loss of empathy, or if he lost other skills (such as the ability to plan).

xv Some people have 'mirror-touch synesthesia' where they consciously feel touched simply by viewing others being touched. These individuals have heightened empathy ability.[63]

xvi This is the so-called P45 electrophysiological response.

xvii Single neurons have been recorded in patients with epilepsy, and in these patients it was recently shown that mirror neurons do exist in the human brain.[70]

xviii Most scientists agree the amygdala has at least two major divisions: the basolateral (BLA) and the central nuclei (CeN). The CeN is involved in programming the response to a conditioned stimulus, while the BLA is involved primarily in the pairing of an emotional tone to a conditioned stimulus. Joe LeDoux and Cambridge neuroscientist Barry Everitt and colleagues demonstrated this in animals.[78, 79]

xix When Joe heard I played in a band too, he suggested we have a jamming session at my house. I invited Bhisma to come along, because we had been studying the brain basis of empathy together. Bhisma plays Indian drums (tabla), Joe plays rhythm guitar. By good fortune, Joe's colleague, neuroscientist Daniela Schiller, is the drummer of the Amgydaloids and she had arrived from her home country of Israel, so she got out her drumsticks. I got out my bass guitar. We had a lot of fun playing music together.

xx Some argue that the posterior cingulate cortex (PCC, or precuneus) and anterior temporal lobe (ATL) are also involved in understanding others' beliefs, so we should keep in mind that the empathy circuit may well ultimately include more than twelve regions.[18, 19, 50, 84, 85]

xxi   See [40, 42, 45, 49, 58–62, 68–71]

xxii   See [19–21, 23–26, 50, 84, 86–89]

xxiii   He was only eleven years old when he had to flee with his family from Nazi Germany, in 1939.

xxiv   Serotonin is a neurotransmitter, also called 5-HT, and it is the 5-HT2A receptor. Type B also show a reduced response to the drug d or d,l fenfluramine that normally triggers serotonin release. And when scientists get the chance to look at the brain of someone who has successfully committed suicide (in post-mortem studies) there are more serotonin receptor binding sites in the prefrontal cortex, but fewer on the pre-synaptic side of nerves that use serotonin (so-called serotinergic nerve terminals). The serotonin system is not the only neurotransmitter abnormality in Type B, as dopamine, norepinephrine, acetylcholine, monoamine oxidase and HPA or thyrotropin-releasing hormone activity have all also been found to be abnormal.

xxv   English has a word that is a bit milder, the verb 'to gloat'.[130]

xxvi   Hervey Cleckley became professor of psychiatry in the University of Georgia Medical School in Augusta in 1937. By coincidence, this was the same year my grandfather's brother, Robert Greenblatt, became professor of endocrinology there.

xxvii   See Bowlby, J., *Attachment* (New York, 1969).

xxviii   See also Harlow, H. and Zimmerman, R., Affectionless responses in the infant monkey. *Science* 130, 431–2 (1959). As an aside, it is interesting as to who judges an experiment as unethical. In Chapter 1 I was clearly condemning of the Nazi experiments that tested how long a person could tolerate freezing water, yet here I seem to be willing to justify Harlow's and Hinde's monkey experiments. I suspect I am guilty of a double standard when it comes to human vs. animal research, and that some would adopt an even more stringent view on the ethics of animal experimentation.

xxix   I remember my first visit to Denmark, a country that has highly developed social care. On the train a whole compartment was set aside as a special play area for young children, with soft toys in bright colours in a special zone where children could be watched by their parents and could feel happy. Trains in my own country of England have no such facilities, possibly because it means giving up seats that could be generating income for the train company. It is worth keeping in mind that whenever you see modifications to our environment that are child-friendly, that these in all likelihood owe their existence to Bowlby's theory. See also Bowlby, J., *Maternal Care and Mental Health* (Geneva, 1951).

xxx The septo-hippocampal system links the septum, the amygdala, the hippocampus and the fornix into a circuit. It is also thought of as the 'behavioural inhibition' circuit and abnormalities in this circuit are linked to anxiety disorders.

xxxi This is a questionnaire devised by Robert Hare. This result was particularly seen on the 'callous' and 'unemotional interpersonal' subscales.

xxxii The basolateral nucleus.

xxxiii The 'mirror neuron hypothesis' of autism is still an area of debate since atypical functioning of this system is not always found in autism.[212, 213]

xxxiv Dopamine and serotonin binding in the vMPFC is also reduced in autism, as is glucose metabolism and regional cerebral blood flow.[222, 223, 224, 225] See Monk, C., et al., Abnormalities of intrinsic functional connectivity in autism spectrum disorders. *Neuroimage* 47, 764–72

xxxv This work has led to the idea that the same underlying neural mechanism causes difficulties both in thinking about one's own mind and someone else's mind. Mike Lombardo tested this and found that the RTPJ/pSTS was under-active in autism during both mentalizing about oneself and for mentalizing about others. Thus, RTPJ/pSTS seems to be a common neural mechanism that could explain 'mindblindness' for self and others.[233]

xxxvi CNR1 has effects on several neurotransmitters (such as dopamine and GABA).

xxxvii The work on foetal testosterone was the subject of an academic monograph I wrote with two of my PhD students, entitled *Prenatal Testosterone In Mind*.[294, 295]

xxxviii Some of these are genes involved in the synthesis of testosterone or oestrogen, others are involved in the transport of these hormones, and yet others are involved in the receptors for these hormones.

xxxix This is involved in making the protein wolframin, needed in many systems throughout the body. Variations in this gene are associated with depression.

xl NTRK1 codes for one of the receptors for neurotrophins that ensure neuronal survival in the developing brain. NTRK1 also plays a role in differentiating sensory neurons.

xli GABRB3 is mutated in a syndrome on the autistic spectrum called Angelman Syndrome and affects the transmission of the neurotransmitter GABA, levels of which influence inhibition of neural activity.

xlii More recent work with mice has shown the involvement of calcium channel genes linked to social learning of fear.[305]

xliii *Daily Telegraph*, 22 June 2001; Mitani, J. C. , Watts, D. P. and Amsler, S. J., Lethal intergroup aggression leads to territorial expansion in wild chimpanzees. *Current Biology* 20 (12), R507–R508 (2010).

xliv See Bateman, A. and Fonagy, P., *Mentalization-based Treatment for Borderline Personality Disorder: A practical guide* (Oxford, 2006).

xlv Also known as De Clerambault's Syndrome.

xlvi The famous example of the latter is how homosexuality was a psychiatric category (a mental illness) in DSM-II, but was dropped in DSM-III in 1973 after gay rights protests at the American Psychiatric Association Conference, and with the recognition that those with a different sexual orientation are not 'ill' and certainly not in need of treatment, as used to be thought.

xlvii See Asch, S., Opinions and Social Pressure. *Scientific American* 193, 21–35 (1955).

xlviii The original quote from Ian Kershaw was 'the road to Auschwitz was built by hate, but paved with indifference'.[328]

xlix Stone's twenty-two types of killers are listed here:

(1) killing in self defence

(2) jealous lovers

(3) willing companions of killers

(4) killing loved ones out of jealousy

(5) drug addicts

(6) hot-headed

(7) Type N

(8) those whose smouldering rage is ignited

(9) jealous lovers with psychopathic features

(10) killing people who are in the way/witnesses

(11) as in 10 but Type P

(12) Type P when cornered

(13) inadequate personalities

(14) Type P 'schemers'

(15) Type P multiple murders

(16) Type P committing multiple vicious acts

(17) Sexually perverse serial murderers, torture-murderers and rapists who murder to hide the evidence

(18) Torture murderers
(19) Other Type P
(20) Type P Torturers
(21) Type P preoccupied with torture, and
(22) Type P serial torture-murderers.

One can see how those at levels 1–8 might have been violent as a result of an extreme *temporary fluctuation* in their state of empathy; those at levels 14–22 might have been violent because of being *permanently unempathic*; with those at levels 9–13 being somewhere in between. If correct, it may be more fruitful to predict two or three levels of degrees of deficit in the empathy circuit among such violent offenders. This is both a more feasible prediction (scanning studies cannot realistically compare twenty-two groups, because of cost, but they can compare three groups), and more likely to be psychologically and neurologically more meaningful. This might correspond to Levels 0–2 of the Empathizing Mechanism (see Chapter 2).

1 There are three well-demonstrated, classical examples of critical or sensitive periods in psychology. First, ethologist Konrad Lorenz demonstrated how newborn chicks would 'imprint' and follow the first thing they saw after hatching from the egg, and that this kind of 'bonding' was irreversible. A second illustration was from vision neuroscientist Colin Blakemore, who demonstrated that depriving a kitten of visual input in the first week of life leads to irreversible forms of cortical blindness because of an interruption of the critical period for the development of visual pathways (including development of sensory receptive fields in the brain). Finally, the third clear demonstration of a critical or sensitive period in development comes from studies of children deprived of language input in the first five to ten years of life, who are less likely to learn language as fluently. See Pinker, S., *The Language Instinct* (London, 1994) and Pinker, S., *The Blank Slate* (London, 2002).

li Peter Sutcliffe was known as the 'Yorkshire Ripper' and convicted in 1981 for murdering thirteen women and attacking others. He was a loner in childhood and was diagnosed with schizophrenia, having heard voices from God and from a graveyard where he worked, telling him to kill the women. Despite his psychiatric diagnosis, he was sentenced to a non-psychiatric prison (Parkhurst), where he was attacked by a fellow prisoner who plunged a broken coffee jar into Sutcliffe's face. After this, Sutcliffe was transferred to the psychiatric prison of Broadmoor under the Mental Health Act. He has also been attacked there at least twice. On 17 February 2009 (according to the *Daily Telegraph*) Sutcliffe was reported to be 'fit to leave Broadmoor'.

lii See Rifkin, J., *The Empathic Civilization* (New York, 2009) and De Waal, F., *The Age of Empathy* (New York, 2009).

liii At www.parentscircle.org you can find many documented examples of this kind from individual families on both the Israeli and Palestinian sides. The names of the individuals given in this example have been changed.

liv The 'Hand in Hand' educational model brings Israeli Arab and Jewish children together in mixed schools to contribute to better mutual understanding (www.handinhandiz.org).

lv Philosopher Daniel Dennett came up with the idea of a 'universal acid', a substance so dangerous that it could not even be kept in a container, as it would corrode anything it touched. (He was referring to the idea of Darwinism as unstoppable, an idea that could penetrate any field.) I think of empathy as the opposite of universal acid, a *universal solvent*. In chemistry, a solution is created when you put something potentially soluble (the solute) into something that can create a solution (the solvent), resulting in the production of a stable equilibrium. Sugar in your tea is an obvious example. See Dennett, D., *Darwin's Dangerous Idea* (New York, 1995).

lvi See Chapman, E., Baron-Cohen, S., Auyeung, B., Knickmeyer, R., Taylor, K. and Hackett, G., Foetal testosterone and empathy: evidence from the Empathy Quotient (EQ) and the 'Reading the Mind in the Eyes' Test. *Social Neuroscience 1*, 135–48 (2006).

lvii Having extreme reactive aggression is not the same as being a psychopath or having Anti-Social Personality Disorder. There is another psychiatric condition with the memorable name 'intermittent explosive disorder' or 'impulsive aggressive disorder'. This is thought to be the result of poor 'executive control' over the regulatory systems that ordinarily dampen down reactive aggression. This is different to the behaviour of psychopaths because the person only shows one 'symptom' (the angry outbursts) without all the other characteristics.

References

1   Baron-Cohen, S., Golan, O., Wheelwright, S. and Hill, J. J., *Mindreading*, DVD (2004, www.jkp.com/mindreading).

2   Baron-Cohen, S., Golan, O., Harcup, C. and Lever, N., *The Transporters*, DVD (2007, www.thetransporters.com).

3   Sapolsky, R. M., *The Trouble With Testosterone and Other Essays on the Human Predicament* (New York, 1997).

4   Bogod, D., The Nazi hypothermia experiments: forbidden data? *Anaesthesia* 59, 1155–6 (2004).

5   *Midweek*, BBC Radio 4, broadcast 14 January 2009.

6   Buergenthal, T., *A Lucky Child: A Memoir of Surviving Auschwitz as a Young Boy* (London, 2009).

7   Buber, M., *I and Thou*, 2nd edn. (New York, 1958).

8   *Guardian*, 28 April 2008.

9   *Whose Justice?*, BBC Newsnight, 28 January 2009.

10 Simonyan, A. and Arzumanyan, M., *Soviet Armenian Encyclopedia* (Yerevan, 1981).

11 Davis, M. H., *Empathy: A Social Psychological Approach* (Colorado, 1994).

12 Baron-Cohen, S. and Wheelwright, S., The Empathy Quotient (EQ). An investigation of adults with Asperger Syndrome or High Functioning Autism, and normal sex differences. *Journal of Autism and Developmental Disorders* 34, 163–75 (2004).

13 Billington, J., Baron-Cohen, S. and Wheelwright, S., Cognitive style predicts entry into physical sciences and humanities: questionnaire and performance tests of empathy and systemizing. *Learning and Individual Differences* 17, 260–8 (2007).

14 Goldenfeld, N., Baron-Cohen, S. and Wheelwright, S., Empathizing and systemizing in males, females and autism. *Clinical Neuropsychiatry* 2, 338–45 (2005).

15 Auyeung, B., Baron-Cohen, S., Wheelwright, S., Samarawickrema, N., Atkinson, M. and Satcher, M., The Children's Empathy Quotient (EQ-C) and Systemizing Quotient (SQ-C): a study of sex differences, typical development and of autism spectrum conditions. *Journal of Autism and Developmental Disorders* 39, 1509–21 (2009).

16 Holliday-Willey, L., *Pretending To Be Normal* (London, 1999).

17 Baron-Cohen, S., *The Essential Difference: Men, Women and the Extreme Male Brain* (London, 2003).

18 Frith, U. and Frith, C., Development and neurophysiology of mentalizing. *Philosophical Transactions of the Royal Society* 358, 459–73 (2003).

19 Amodio, D. M. and Frith, C. D., Meeting of minds: the medial frontal cortex and social cognition. *Nature Reviews Neuroscience* 7, 268–77 (2006).

20 Mitchell, J. P., Macrae, C. N. and Banaji, M. R., Dissociable medial prefrontal contributions to judgments of similar and dissimilar others. *Neuron* 50, 655–63 (2006).

21 Ochsner, K. N., Beer, J. S., Robertson, E. R., Cooper, J. C., Gabrieli, J. D., Kihsltrom, J. F. and D'Esposito, M., The neural correlates of direct and reflected self-knowledge. *Neuroimage* 28 (4), 797–814 (2005).

22 Coricelli, G. and Nagel, R., Neural correlates of depth of strategic reasoning in medial prefrontal cortex. *Proceedings of the National Academy of Sciences of the United States of America* 106, 9163–8 (2009).

23 Ochsner, K. N., Knierim, K., Ludlow, D. H., Hanelin, J., Ramachandran, T., Glover, G. and Mackey, S. C., Reflecting upon feelings: an fMRI study of neural systems supporting the attribution of emotion to self and other. *Journal of Cognitive Neuroscience* 16, 1746–72 (2004).

24 Lombardo, M. V., Chakrabarti, B., Bullmore, E. T., Wheelwright, S. J., Sadek, S. A., Suckling, J. and Baron-Cohen, S., Shared neural circuits for mentalizing about the self and others. *Journal of Cognitive Neuroscience* 22, 1623–35 (2010).

25 Jenkins, A. C., Macrae, C. N. and Mitchell, J. P., Repetition suppression of ventromedial prefrontal activity during judgments of self and others. *Proceedings of the National Academy of Sciences of the United States of America* 105, 4507–12 (2008).

26 Moran, J. M., Macrae, C. N., Heatherton, T. F., Wyland, C. L. and Kelley, W. M., Neuroanatomical evidence for distinct cognitive and

affective components of self. *Journal of Cognitive Neuroscience* 18, 1586–94 (2006).

27 Sharot, T., Riccardi, A. M., Raio, C. M. and Phelps, E. A., Neural mechanisms mediating optimism bias. *Nature* 450, 102–5 (2007).

28 Mayberg, H. S., Lozano, A. M., Voon, V., McNeely, H. E., Seminowicz, D., Hamani, C., Schwalb, J. M. and Kennedy, S. H., Deep brain stimulation for treatment-resistant depression. *Neuron* 45, 651–60 (2005).

29 Beer, J. S., Heerey, E. A., Keltner, D., Scabini, D. and Knight, R. T., The regulatory function of self-conscious emotion: insights from patients with orbitofrontal damage. *Journal of Personality and Social Psychology* 85, 594–604 (2003).

30 Beer, J. S., John, O. P., Scabini, D. and Knight, R. T., Orbitofrontal cortex and social behavior: integrating self-monitoring and emotion-cognition interactions. *Journal of Cognitive Neuroscience* 18, 871–9 (2006).

31 Shamay-Tsoory, S. G., Aharon-Peretz, J. and Perry, D., Two systems for empathy: a double dissociation between emotional and cognitive empathy in inferior frontal gyrus versus ventromedial prefrontal lesions. *Brain* 132, 617–27 (2009).

32 Damasio, H., Grabowski, T., Frank, R., Galaburda, A. M. and Damasio, A. R., The return of Phineas Gage: clues about the brain from the skull of a famous patient. *Science* 264, 1102–5 (1994).

33 Macmillan, M., Restoring Phineas Gage: a 150th retrospective. *Journal of the History of the Neurosciences* 9, 46–66 (2000).

34 Baron-Cohen, S., Ring, H., Moriarty, J., Shmitz, P., Costa, D. and Ell, P., Recognition of mental state terms: a clinical study of autism, and a functional neuroimaging study of normal adults. *British Journal of Psychiatry* 165, 640–9 (1994).

35 Stone, V., Baron-Cohen, S. and Knight, K., Frontal lobe contributions to theory of mind. *Journal of Cognitive Neuroscience* 10, 640–56 (1998).

36 Lamm, C., Nusbaum, H. C., Meltzoff, A. N. and Decety, J., What are you feeling? Using functional magnetic resonance imaging to assess the modulation of sensory and affective responses during empathy for pain. *Public Library of Science One* 2, e1292 (2007).

37 Kumar, P., Waiter, G., Ahearn, T., Milders, M., Reid, I. and Steele, J. D., Frontal operculum temporal difference signals and social motor response learning. *Human Brain Mapping* 30, 1421–30 (2008).

38 Calder, A. J., Lawrence, A. D. and Young, A. W., Neuropsychology of fear and loathing. *Nature Reviews Neuroscience* 2, 352–63 (2001).

39 Chakrabarti, B., Bullmore, E. T. and Baron-Cohen, S., Empathizing with basic emotions: common and discrete neural substrates. *Social Neuroscience* 1, 364–84 (2006).

40 Hutchison, W. D., Davis, K. D., Lozano, A. M., Tasker, R. R. and Dostrovsky, J. O., Pain-related neurons in the human cingulate cortex. *Nature Neuroscience* 2, 403–5 (1999).

41 Craig, A. D., How do you feel—now? The anterior insula and human awareness. *Nature Reviews Neuroscience* 10, 59–70 (2009).

42 Singer, T., Seymour, B., O'Doherty, J., Kaube, H., Dolan, R. J. and Frith, C. D., Empathy for pain involves the affective but not sensory components of pain. *Science* 303, 1157–67 (2004).

43 Jackson, P. L., Meltzoff, A. N. and Decety, J., How do we perceive the pain of others? A window into the neural processes involved in empathy. *Neuroimage* 24, 771–9 (2005).

44 Lamm, C., Batson, C. D. and Decety, J., The neural substrate of human empathy: effects of perspective-taking and cognitive appraisal. *Journal of Cognitive Neuroscience* 19, 42–58 (2007).

45 Wicker, B., Keysers, C., Plailly, J., Royet, J. P., Gallese, V. and Rizzolatti, G., Both of us disgusted in my insula: The common neural basis of seeing and feeling disgust. *Neuron* 40, 655–64 (2003).

46 Singer, T., Seymour, B., O'Doherty, J. P., Stephan, K. E., Dolan, R. J. and Frith, C. D., Empathic neural responses are modulated by the perceived fairness of others. *Nature* 439, 466–9 (2006).

47 Carr, L. M., Iacoboni, M., Dubeau, M.-C., Mazziotta, J. and Lenzi, G., Neural mechanisms of empathy in humans: A relay from neural systems for imitation to limbic areas. *Proceedings of the National Academy of Sciences of the United States of America* 100, 5497–502 (2003).

48 Jabbi, M., Swart, M. and Keysers, C., Empathy for positive and negative emotions in the gustatory cortex. *Neuroimage* 34, 1744–53 (2007).

49 Morrison, I., Lloyd, D., di Pellegrino, G. and Roberts, N., Vicarious responses to pain in anterior cingulate cortex: is empathy a multisensory issue? *Cognitive Affective and Behavioural Neuroscience* 4, 270–8 (2004).

50 Saxe, R. and Kanwisher, N., People thinking about thinking people. The role of the temporo-parietal junction in 'theory of mind'. *Neuroimage* 19, 1835–42 (2003).

51 Blanke, O. and Arzy, S., The out-of-body experience: disturbed self-processing at the temporo-parietal junction. *Neuroscientist* 11, 16–24 (2005).

52 Arzy, S., Seeck, M., Ortigue, S., Spinelli, L. and Blanke, O., Induction of an illusory shadow person. *Nature* 443, 287 (2006).

53 Scholtz, J., Triantafyllou, C., Whitfield-Gabrieli, S., Brown, E. N. and Saxe, R., Distinct regions of right temporo-parietal junction are selective for theory of mind and exogenous attention. *Public Library of Science One* 4, e4869 (2009).

54 Decety, J. and Lamm, C., The role of the right temporoparietal junction in social interaction: how low-level computational processes contribute to meta-cognition. *Neuroscientist* 13, 580–93 (2007).

55 Campbell, R., Heywood, C., Cowey, A., Regard, M. and Landis, T., Sensitivity to eye gaze in prosopagnosic patients and monkeys with superior temporal sulcus ablation. *Neuropsychologia* 28, 1123–42 (1990).

56 Baron-Cohen, S., Jolliffe, T., Mortimore, C. and Robertson, M., Another advanced test of theory of mind: evidence from very high functioning adults with autism or Asperger Syndrome. *Journal of Child Psychology and Psychiatry* 38, 813–22 (1997).

57 Grossman, E. D. and Blake, R., Brain activity evoked by inverted and imagined biological motion. *Vision Research* 41, 1475–82 (2001).

58 Keysers, C., Kaas, J. H. and Gazzola, V., Somatosensation in social perception. *Nature Reviews Neuroscience* 11, 417–28 (2010).

59 Keysers, C., Wicker, B., Gazzola, V., Anton, J. L., Fogassi, L. and Gallese, V., A touching sight: SII/PV activation during the observation and experience of touch. *Neuron* 42, 335–46 (2004).

60 Blakemore, S. J., Bristow, D., Bird, G., Frith, C. and Ward, J., Somatosensory activations during the observation of touch and a case of vision-touch synaesthesia. *Brain* 128, 1571–83 (2005).

61 Ebisch, S. J., Perrucci, M. G., Ferretti, A., Del Gratta, C., Romani, G. L. and Gallese, V., The sense of touch: embodied simulation in a visuo-tactile mirroring mechanism for observed animate or inanimate touch. *Journal of Cognitive Neuroscience* 20, 1611–23 (2008).

62 Ishida, H., Nakajima, K., Inase, M. and Murata, A., Shared mapping of own and others' bodies in visuotactile bimodal area of monkey parietal cortex. *Journal of Cognitive Neuroscience* 22, 83–96 (2010).

63 Banissy, M. J. and Ward, J., Mirror-touch synesthesia is linked with empathy. *Nature Neuroscience* 10, 815–16 (2007).

64 Bufalari, I., Aprile, T., Avenanti, A., Di Russo, F. and Aglioti, S. M.,

Empathy for pain and touch in the human somatosensory cortex. *Cerebral Cortex* **17**, 2553–61 (2007).

65 Adolphs, R., Damasio, H., Tranel, D., Cooper, G. and Damasio, A. R., A role for somatosensory cortices in the visual recognition of emotion as revealed by three-dimensional lesion mapping. *Journal of Neuroscience* **20**, 2683–90 (2000).

66 Pitcher, D., Garrido, L., Walsh, V. and Duchaine, B. C., Transcranial magnetic stimulation disrupts the perception and embodiment of facial expressions. *Journal of Neuroscience* **28**, 8929–33 (2008).

67 Cheng, Y., Lin, C. P., Liu, H. L., Hsu, Y. Y., Lim, K. E., Hung, D. and Decety, J., Expertise modulates the perception of pain in others. *Current Biology* **17**, 1708–13 (2007).

68 Rizzolatti, G. and Craighero, L., The mirror-neuron system. *Annual Review in Neuroscience* **27**, 169–92 (2004).

69 Dapretto, M., Davies, M. S., Pfeifer, J. H., Scott, A. A., Sigman, M., Bookheimer, S. Y. and Iacoboni, M., Understanding emotions in others: mirror neuron dysfunction in children with autism spectrum disorders. *Nature Neuroscience* **9**, 28–30 (2006).

70 Mukamel, R., Ekstrom, A. D., Kaplan, J., Iacoboni, M. and Fried, I., Single-neuron responses in humans during execution and observation of actions. *Current Biology* **20**, 750–6 (2010).

71 Shepherd, S. V., Klein, J. T., Deaner, R. O. and Platt, M. L., Mirroring of attention by neurons in macaque parietal cortex. *Proceedings of the National Academy of Sciences of the United States of America* **106**, 9489–94 (2009).

72 Chartrand, T. L. and Bargh, J. A., The chameleon effect: the perception-behavior link and social interaction. *Journal of Personality and Social Psychology* **76**, 893–910 (1999).

73 Zaki, J., Weber, J., Bolger, N. and Ochsner, K., The neural bases of empathic accuracy. *Proceedings of the National Academy of Sciences of the United States of America* **106**, 11382–7 (2009).

74 Schippers, M. B., Roebroeck, A., Renken, R., Nanetti, L. and Keysers, C., Mapping the information flow from one brain to another during gestural communication. *Proceedings of the National Academy of Sciences of the United States of America* **107**, 9388–93 (2010).

75 Lee, K. H. and Siegle, G. J., Common and distinct brain networks underlying explicit emotional evaluation: a meta-analytic study. *Social Cognitive and Affective Neuroscience* published online on 6 March 2009.

76 Wager, T. D., Davidson, M. L., Hughes, B. L., Lindquist, M. A. and

Ochsner, K. N., Prefrontal-subcortical pathways mediating successful emotion regulation. *Neuron* 59, 1037–50 (2008).

77 LeDoux, J. E., *The Emotional Brain: The Mysterious Underpinnings of Emotional Life* (London, 1998).

78 Everitt, B. J., Cardinal, R. N., Parkinson, J. A. and Robbins, T. W., Appetitive behavior: impact of amygdala-dependent mechanisms of emotional learning. *Annals of the New York Academy of Sciences* 985, 233–50 (2003).

79 Johansen, J. P., Hamanaka, H., Monfils, M. H., Behnia, R., Deisseroth, K., Blair, H. T. and LeDoux, J. E., Optical activation of lateral amygdala pyramidal cells instructs associative fear learning. *Proceedings of the National Academy of Sciences of the United States of America* 107, 12692–7 (2010).

80 Baron-Cohen, S., Ring, H., Wheelwright, S., Bullmore, E. T., Brammer, M. J., Simmons, A. and Williams, S., Social intelligence in the normal and autistic brain: an fMRI study. *European Journal of Neuroscience* 11, 1891–8 (1999).

81 Adolphs, R., Tranel, D., Damasio, H. and Damasio, A. R., Fear and the human amygdala. *Journal of Neuroscience* 15, 5879–91 (1995).

82 Spezio, M. L., Huang, P. Y., Castelli, F. and Adolphs, R., Amygdala damage impairs eye contact during conversations with real people. *Journal of Neuroscience* 27, 3994–7 (2007).

83 Adolphs, R., Gosselin, F., Buchanan, T. W., Tranel, D., Schyns, P. and Damasio, A. R., A mechanism for impaired fear recognition after amygdala damage. *Nature* 433, 68–72 (2005).

84 Fletcher, P. C., Happe, F., Frith, U., Baker, S. C., Dolan, R. J., Frackowiak, R. S. J. and Frith, C. D., Other minds in the brain: a functional imaging study of 'theory of mind' in story comprehension. *Cognition* 57, 109–28 (1995).

85 Saxe, R. and Powell, L. J., It's the thought that counts: specific brain regions for one component of theory of mind. *Psychological Science* 17, 692–9 (2006).

86 Gusnard, D. A., Akbudak, E., Shulman, G. L. and Raichle, M. E., Medial prefrontal cortex and self-referential mental activity: relation to a default mode of brain function. *Proceedings of the National Academy of Sciences of the United States of America* 98, 4259–64 (2001).

87 Johnson, S. C., Baxter, L. C., Wilder, L. S., Pipe, J. G., Heiserman, J. E. and Prigatano, G. P., Neural correlates of self-reflection. *Brain* 125, 1808–14 (2002).

88 Kelley, W. M., Macrae, C. N., Wyland, C. L., Caglar, S., Inati, S. and Heatherton, T. F., Finding the self? An event-related fMRI study. *Journal of Cognitive Neuroscience* 14, 785–94 (2002).

89 Northoff, G., Heinzel, A., de Greck, M., Bermpohl, F., Dobrowolny, H. and Panksepp, J., Self-referential processing in our brain: a meta-analysis of imaging studies on the self. *Neuroimage* 31 (1), 440–57 (2006).

90 Kreisman, J. J. and Straus, H., *I Hate You, Don't Leave Me: Understanding The Borderline Personality* (New York, 1989).

91 Johnson, C., Tobin, D. and Enright, A., Prevalence and clinical characteristics of borderline patients in an eating-disordered population. *Journal of Clinical Psychiatry* 50, 9–15 (1989).

92 Nace, E. P., Saxon, J. J., Jr. and Shore, N., A comparison of borderline and nonborderline alcoholic patients. *Archives of General Psychiatry* 40, 54–6 (1983).

93 Inman, D. J., Bascue, L. O. and Skoloda, T., Identification of borderline personality disorders among substance abuse inpatients. *Journal of Substance Abuse Treatment* 2, 229–32 (1985).

94 Soloff, P. H., Lis, J. A., Kelly, T., Cornelius, J. and Ulrich, R., Risk factors for suicidal behavior in borderline personality disorder. *American Journal of Psychiatry* 151, 1316–23 (1994).

95 Zisook, S., Goff, A., Sledge, P. and Shuchter, S. R., Reported suicidal behavior and current suicidal ideation in a psychiatric outpatient clinic. *Annals of Clinical Psychiatry* 6, 27–31 (1994).

96 Isomesta, E. T., Henriksson, M. M., Heikkinen, M. E., Aro, H. M., Marttunen, M. J., Kuoppasalmi, K. I. and Lonnqvist, J. K., Suicide among subjects with personality disorders. *American Journal of Psychiatry* 153, 667–73 (1996).

97 Runeson, B., Mental disorder in youth suicide. DSM-III-R Axes I and II. *Acta Psychiatrica Scandinavica* 79, 490–7 (1989).

98 Paris, J. and Zweig-Frank, H., A 27-year follow-up of patients with borderline personality disorder. *Comprehensive Psychiatry* 42, 482–7 (2001).

99 Stone, M. H., Stone, D. K. and Hurt, S. W., Natural history of borderline patients treated by intensive hospitalization. *Psychiatric Clinics of North America* 10, 185–206 (1987).

100 Rosten, N., *Marilyn, An Untold Story* (New York, 1973).

101 Gunderson, J. G., Kerr, J. and Englund, D. W., The families of borderlines. A comparative study. *Archives of General Psychiatry* 37, 27–33 (1980).

102 Frank, H. and Paris, J., Recollections of family experience in border-line patients. *Archives of General Psychiatry* **38**, 1031–4 (1981).

103 Ogata, S. N., Silk, K. R., Goodrich, S., Lohr, N. E., Westen, D. and Hill, E. M., Childhood sexual and physical abuse in adult patients with borderline personality disorder. *American Journal of Psychiatry* **147**, 1008–13 (1990).

104 Paris, J., Zweig-Frank, H. and Guzder, J., Risk factors for borderline personality in male outpatients. *Journal of Nervous and Mental Disease* **182**, 375–80 (1994).

105 Zanarini, M. C., Childhood experiences associated with the development of borderline personality disorder. *Psychiatric Clinics of North America* **23**, 89–101 (2000).

106 Zweig-Frank, H., Paris, J. and Guzder, J., Psychological risk factors for dissociation and self-mutilation in female patients with borderline personality disorder. *Canadian Journal of Psychiatry* **39**, 259–64 (1994).

107 Yen, S., Zlotnick, C. and Costello, E., Affect regulation in women with borderline personality disorder traits. *Journal of Nervous and Mental Disease* **190**, 693–6 (2002).

108 Bandelow, B., Krause, J., Wedekind, D., Broocks, A., Hajak, G. and Ruther, E., Early traumatic life events, parental attitudes, family history, and birth risk factors in patients with borderline personality disorder and healthy controls. *Psychiatry Research* **134**, 169–79 (2005).

109 New, A. S., Triebwasser, J. and Charney, D. S., The case for shifting borderline personality disorder to Axis I. *Biological Psychiatry* **64**, 653–9 (2008).

110 Paris, J., Nowlis, D. and Brown, R., Developmental factors in the outcome of borderline personality disorder. *Comprehensive Psychiatry* **29**, 147–50 (1988).

111 Bryer, J. B., Nelson, B. A., Miller, J. B. and Krol, P. A., Childhood sexual and physical abuse as factors in adult psychiatric illness. *American Journal of Psychiatry* **144**, 1426–30 (1987).

112 Soloff, P. H., Price, J. C., Meltzer, C. C., Fabio, A., Frank, G. K. and Kaye, W. H., 5HT2A receptor binding is increased in borderline personality disorder. *Biological Psychiatry* **62**, 580–7 (2007).

113 Snyder, S. and Pitts, W. M., Jr., Electroencephalography of DSM-III borderline personality disorder. *Acta Psychiatrica Scandinavica* **69**, 129–34 (1984).

114 Soloff, P. H., Kelly, T. M., Strotmeyer, S. J., Malone, K. M. and Mann,

J. J., Impulsivity, gender, and response to fenfluramine challenge in borderline personality disorder. *Psychiatry Research* 119, 11–24 (2003).

115 Siever, L. J., Buchsbaum, M. S., New, A. S., Spiegel-Cohen, J., Wei, T., Hazlett, E. A., Sevin, E., Nunn, M. and Mitropoulou, V., d,l-fenfluramine response in impulsive personality disorder assessed with [18F] fluorodeoxyglucose positron emission tomography. *Neuropsychopharmacology* 20, 413–23 (1999).

116 Soloff, P. H., Meltzer, C. C., Greer, P. J., Constantine, D. and Kelly, T. M., A fenfluramine-activated FDG-PET study of borderline personality disorder. *Biological Psychiatry* 47, 540–7 (2000).

117 Arango, V., Underwood, M. D., Gubbi, A. V. and Mann, J. J., Localized alterations in pre- and postsynaptic serotonin binding sites in the ventrolateral prefrontal cortex of suicide victims. *Brain Research* 688, 121–33 (1995).

118 Stockmeier, C. A., Dilley, G. E., Shapiro, L. A., Overholser, J. C., Thompson, P. A. and Meltzer, H. Y., Serotonin receptors in suicide victims with major depression. *Neuropsychopharmacology* 16, 162–73 (1997).

119 Juengling, F. D., Schmahl, C., Hesslinger, B., Ebert, D., Bremner, J. D., Gostomzyk, J., Bohus, M. and Lieb, K., Positron emission tomography in female patients with borderline personality disorder. *Journal of Psychiatric Research* 37, 109–15 (2003).

120 Herpertz, S. C., Dietrich, T. M., Wenning, B., Krings, T., Erberich, S. G., Willmes, K., Thron, A. and Sass, H., Evidence of abnormal amygdala functioning in borderline personality disorder: a functional MRI study. *Biological Psychiatry* 50, 292–8 (2001).

121 Donegan, N. H., Sanislow, C. A., Blumberg, H. P., Fulbright, R. K., Lacadie, C., Skudlarski, P., Gore, J. C., Olson, I. R., McGlashan, T. H. and Wexler, B. E., Amygdala hyperreactivity in borderline personality disorder: implications for emotional dysregulation. *Biological Psychiatry* 54, 1284–93 (2003).

122 King-Casas, B., Sharp, C., Lomax-Bream, L., Lohrenz, T., Fonagy, P. and Montague, P. R., The rupture and repair of cooperation in borderline personality disorder. *Science* 321, 806–10 (2008).

123 Brambilla, P., Soloff, P. H., Sala, M., Nicoletti, M. A., Keshavan, M. S. and Soares, J. C., Anatomical MRI study of borderline personality disorder patients. *Psychiatry Research* 131, 125–33 (2004).

124 Driessen, M., Herrmann, J., Stahl, K., Zwaan, M., Meier, S., Hill, A., Osterheider, M. and Petersen, D., Magnetic resonance imaging

volumes of the hippocampus and the amygdala in women with borderline personality disorder and early traumatization. *Archives of General Psychiatry* 57, 1115–22 (2000).

125 Rusch, N., van Elst, L. T., Ludaescher, P., Wilke, M., Huppertz, H. J., Thiel, T., Schmahl, C., Bohus, M., Lieb, K., Hesslinger, B., Hennig, J. and Ebert, D., A voxel-based morphometric MRI study in female patients with borderline personality disorder. *Neuroimage* 20, 385–92 (2003).

126 van Elst, L. T., Hesslinger, B., Thiel, T., Geiger, E., Haegele, K., Lemieux, L., Lieb, K., Bohus, M., Hennig, J. and Ebert, D., Frontolimbic brain abnormalities in patients with borderline personality disorder: a volumetric magnetic resonance imaging study. *Biological Psychiatry* 54, 163–71 (2003).

127 Soloff, P. H., Fabio, A., Kelly, T. M., Malone, K. M. and Mann, J. J., High-lethality status in patients with borderline personality disorder. *Journal of Personality Disorders* 19, 386–99 (2005).

128 Fertuck, E. A., Jekal, A., Song, I., Wyman, B., Morris, M. C., Wilson, S. T., Brodsky, B. S. and Stanley, B., Enhanced 'Reading the Mind in the Eyes' in borderline personality disorder compared to healthy controls. *Psychological Medicine* 39, 1979–88 (2009).

129 Fertuck, E. A., Lenzenweger, M. F., Clarkin, J. F., Hoermann, S. and Stanley, B., Executive neurocognition, memory systems, and borderline personality disorder. *Clinical Psychology Review* 26, 346–75 (2006).

130 Shamay-Tsoory, S. G., Tibi-Elhanany, Y. and Aharon-Peretz, J., The green-eyed monster and malicious joy: the neuroanatomical bases of envy and gloating (schadenfreude). *Brain* 130, 1663–78 (2007).

131 American Psychiatric Association, DSM-IV *Diagnostic and Statistical Manual of Mental Disorders*, 4th edition (Washington, DC, 1994).

132 Fazel, S. and Danesh, J., Serious mental disorder in 23000 prisoners: a systematic review of 62 surveys. *Lancet* 359, 545–50 (2002).

133 Hart, S. D. and Hare, R. D., Psychopathy and antisocial personality disorder. *Current Opinion in Psychiatry* 9, 129–32 (1996).

134 Cleckley, H. M., *The Mask of Sanity*, rev. edn. (New York, 1982).

135 Babiak, P. and Hare, R. D., *Snakes In Suits: When Psychopaths Go to Work* (New York, 2007).

136 Christie, R. and Geis, F. L., *Studies in Machiavellianism* (New York, 1970).

137 Rutter, M., Psychosocial resilience and protective mechanisms. *American Journal of Orthopsychiatry* 57, 316–31 (1987).

138 Saltaris, C., Psychopathy in juvenile offenders. Can temperament and attachment be considered as robust developmental precursors? *Clinical Psychology Reviews* 22, 729–52 (2002).

139 DeKlyen, M., Speltz, M. L. and Greenberg, M. T., Fathering and early onset conduct problems: positive and negative parenting, father–son attachment, and the marital context. *Clinical Child and Family Psychology Review* 1, 3–21 (1998).

140 Hinde, R. A. and Spencer-Booth, Y., Effects of brief separation from mother on rhesus monkeys. *Science* 173, 111–18 (1971).

141 Harris, P., *Children and Emotions* (London, 1989).

142 Marshall, L. A. and Cooke, D. J., The childhood experiences of psychopaths: a retrospective study of familial and societal factors. *Journal of Personality Disorders* 13, 211–25 (1999).

143 Fonagy, P., Attachment and borderline personality disorder. *Journal of the American Psychoanalytical Association* 48, 1129–46; discussion 1175–87 (2000).

144 Baumrind, D., Rejoinder to Lewis' reinterpretation of parental firm control effects: Are authoritative families really harmonious? *Psychological Bulletin* 94, 132–42 (1983).

145 Davis, M. H., Measuring individual differences in empathy: evidence for a multidimensional approach. *Journal of Personality and Social Psychology* 44, 113–26 (1983).

146 Blair, R. J. R., Responsiveness to distress cues in the child with psychopathic tendencies. *Personality and Individual Differences* 27, 135–45 (1999).

147 Blair, R. J. R., Moral reasoning in the child with psychopathic tendencies. *Personality and Individual Differences* 22, 731–9 (1997).

148 Blair, R. J. R. and Coles, M., Expression recognition and behavioural problems in early adolescence. *Cognitive Development* 15, 421–34 (2000).

149 Stevens, D., Charman, T. and Blair, R. J. R., Recognition of emotion in facial expressions and vocal tones in children with psychopathic tendencies. *Journal of Genetic Psychology* 162, 201–11 (2001).

150 Lorenz, A. R. and Newman, J. P., Deficient response modulation and emotion processing in low-anxious Caucasian psychopathic offenders: results from a lexical decision task. *Emotion* 2, 91–104 (2002).

151 Williamson, S., Harpur, T. J. and Hare, R. D., Abnormal processing of affective words by psychopaths. *Psychophysiology* 28, 260–73 (1991).

152 Dodge, K. A., Social-cognitive mechanisms in the development of

conduct disorder and depression. *Annual Review of Psychology* 44, 559–84 (1993).

153 Lee, M. and Prentice, N. M., Interrelations of empathy, cognition, and moral reasoning with dimensions of juvenile delinquency. *Journal of Abnormal Child Psychology* 16, 127–39 (1988).

154 Smetana, J. G. and Braeges, J. L., The development of toddlers' moral and conventional judgments. *Merrill-Palmer Quarterly* 36, 329–46 (1990).

155 Dunn, J. and Hughes, C., 'I got some swords and you're dead!': violent fantasy, antisocial behavior, friendship, and moral sensibility in young children. *Child Development* 72, 491–505 (2001).

156 Gray, J. A., *The Neuropsychology of Anxiety: An Enquiry into the Functions of the Septo-Hippocampal System* (Oxford, 1982).

157 Newman, J. P., Psychopathic behaviour: an information processing perpective, in *Psychopathy: Theory, Research and Implications for Society*, edited by Cooke, D. J., Forth, A. E. and Hare, R. D. (Dordrecht, 1998), pp. 81–104.

158 Newman, J. P., Patterson, C. M. and Kosson, D. S., Response perseveration in psychopaths. *Journal of Abnormal Psychology* 96, 145–8 (1987).

159 Hoffman, M. L., Discipline and internalization. *Developmental Psychology* 30, 26–8 (1994).

160 Cleckley, H. M., *The Mask of Sanity: An Attempt to Clarify Some Issues about the So-Called Psychopathic Personality*, 5th edn. (St Louis, 1976).

161 Verona, E., Patrick, C. J. and Joiner, T. E., Psychopathy, antisocial personality, and suicide risk. *Journal of Abnormal Psychology* 110, 462–70 (2001).

162 Lykken, D. T., A study of anxiety in the sociopathic personality. *Journal of Abnormal and Social Psychology* 55, 6–10 (1957).

163 Flor, H., Birbaumer, N., Hermann, C., Ziegler, S. and Patrick, C. J., Aversive Pavlovian conditioning in psychopaths: peripheral and central correlates. *Psychophysiology* 39 (4), 505–18 (2002).

164 Levenston, G. K., Patrick, C. J., Bradley, M. M. and Lang, P. J., The psychopath as observer: emotion and attention in picture processing. *Journal of Abnormal Psychology* 109 (3), 373–85 (2000).

165 Volkow, N. D. and Tancredi, L., Neural substrates of violent behaviour. A preliminary study with positron emission tomography. *British Journal of Psychiatry* 151, 668–73 (1987).

166 Soderstrom, H., Hultin, L., Tullberg, M., Wikkelso, C., Ekholm, S. and

Forsman, A., Reduced frontotemporal perfusion in psychopathic personality. *Psychiatry Research* 114, 81–94 (2002).

167 Craig, M. C., Catani, M., Deeley, Q., Latham, R., Daly, E., Kanaan, R., Picchioni, M., McGuire, P. K., Fahy, T. and Murphy, D. G., Altered connections on the road to psychopathy. *Molecular Psychiatry* 14, 946–53, (2009).

168 Raine, A., Yang, Y., Narr, K. L. and Toga, A. W., Sex differences in orbitofrontal gray as a partial explanation for sex differences in antisocial personality. *Molecular Psychiatry* (Epub ahead of print, 22 December 2009).

169 Damasio, A. R., Tranel, D. and Damasio, H. C., Individuals with sociopathic behavior caused by frontal damage fail to respond autonomically to social stimuli. *Behavioral Brain Research* 41, 81–94 (1990).

170 Damasio, A. R., Tranel, D. and Damasio, H. C., Somatic markers and the guidance of behavior: theory and preliminary testing, in *Frontal Lobe Function and Dysfunction*, edited by H. S. Levin, H. M. Eisenberg and A. L. Benton (New York, 1991).

171 Krajbich, I., Adolphs, R., Tranel, D., Denburg, N. L. and Camerer, C. F., Economic games quantify diminished sense of guilt in patients with damage to the prefrontal cortex. *Journal of Neuroscience* 29, 2188–92 (2009).

172 Koenigs, M., Young, L., Adolphs, R., Tranel, D., Cushman, F., Hauser, M. and Damasio, A., Damage to the prefrontal cortex increases utilitarian moral judgements. *Nature* 446, 908–11 (2007).

173 Young, L., Bechara, A., Tranel, D., Damasio, H., Hauser, M. and Damasio, A., Damage to ventromedial prefrontal cortex impairs judgment of harmful intent. *Neuron* 65, 845–51 (2010).

174 Heims, H. C., Critchley, H. D., Dolan, R., Mathias, C. J. and Cipolotti, L., Social and motivational functioning is not critically dependent on feedback of autonomic responses: neuropsychological evidence from patients with pure autonomic failure. *Neuropsychologia* 42, 1979–88 (2004).

175 Damasio, A. R., *Descartes' Error: Emotion, Rationality and the Human Brain* (New York, 1994).

176 Raine, A., Buchsbaum, M. and LaCasse, L., Brain abnormalities in murderers indicated by positron emission tomography. *Biological Psychiatry* 42, 495–508 (1997).

177 Raine, A., Lencz, T., Bihrle, S., LaCasse, L. and Colletti, P., Reduced prefrontal gray matter volume and reduced autonomic activity in

antisocial personality disorder. *Archives of General Psychiatry* 57, 119–27; discussion 128–9 (2000).

178 Goyer, P. F., Andreason, P. J., Semple, W. E., Clayton, A. H., King, A. C., Compton-Toth, B. A., Schulz, S. C. and Cohen, R. M., Positron-emission tomography and personality disorders. *Neuropsychopharmacology* 10, 21–8 (1994).

179 Buckholtz, J. W., Treadway, M. T., Cowan, R. L., Woodward, N. D., Benning, S. D., Li, R., Ansari, M. S., Baldwin, R. M., Schwartzman, A. N., Shelby, E. S., Smith, C. E., Cole, D., Kessler, R. M. and Zald, D. H., Mesolimbic dopamine reward system hypersensitivity in individuals with psychopathic traits. *Nature Neuroscience* 13, 419–21 (2010).

180 Young, L., Camprodon, J. A., Hauser, M., Pascual-Leone, A. and Saxe, R., Disruption of the right temporoparietal junction with transcranial magnetic stimulation reduces the role of beliefs in moral judgments. *Proceedings of the National Academy of Sciences of the United States of America* 107, 6753–8 (2010).

181 Young, L., Cushman, F., Hauser, M. and Saxe, R., The neural basis of the interaction between theory of mind and moral judgment. *Proceedings of the National Academy of Sciences of the United States of America* 104, 8235–40 (2007).

182 Decety, J., Michalska, K. J., Akitsuki, Y. and Lahey, B. B., Atypical empathic responses in adolescents with aggressive conduct disorder: a functional MRI investigation. *Biological Psychology* 80, 203–11 (2009).

183 Veit, R., Flor, H., Erb, M., Hermann, C., Lotze, M., Grodd, W. and Birbaumer, N., Brain circuits involved in emotional learning in antisocial behavior and social phobia in humans. *Neuroscience Letters* 328, 233–6 (2002).

184 Bremner, J. D., Randall, P., Scott, T. M., Capelli, S., Delaney, R., McCarthy, G., and Charney, D. S., Deficits in short-term memory in adult survivors of childhood abuse. *Psychiatry Research* 59, 97–107 (1995).

185 Panksepp, J., *Affective Neuroscience: The Foundations of Human and Animal Emotions* (New York, 1998).

186 Jacobson, L. and Sapolsky, R., The role of the hippocampus in feedback regulation of the hypothalamic-pituitary-adrenocortical axis. *Endocrine Reviews* 12, 118–34 (1991).

187 McEwen, B. S., Angulo, J., Cameron, H., Chao, H. M., Daniels, D., Gannon, M. N., Gould, E., Mendelson, S., Sakai, R. and Spencer, R. Paradoxical effects of adrenal steroids on the brain: protection versus degeneration. *Biological Psychiatry* 31, 177–99 (1992).

188 Vyas, A., Mitra, R., Shankaranarayana Rao, B. S. and Chattarji, S.,

Chronic stress induces contrasting patterns of dendritic remodeling in hippocampal and amygdaloid neurons. *Journal of Neuroscience* 22, 6810–18 (2002).

189 Drevets, W. C., Neuroimaging abnormalities in the amygdala in mood disorders. *Annals of the New York Academy of Sciences* 985, 420–44 (2003).

190 Hettema, J. M., Neale, M. C. and Kendler, K. S., A review and meta-analysis of the genetic epidemiology of anxiety disorders. *American Journal of Psychiatry* 158, 1568–78 (2001).

191 Blair, R. J. R., Mitchell, D. and Blair, K., *The Psychopath: Emotion and the Brain* (Oxford, 2005).

192 Stone, M. H., Normal narcissism: an etiological and ethological perspective, in *Disorders of Narcissism: Diagnostic, Clinical and Empirical Implications*, edited by E. F. Ronningstram (Washington, DC, 1997), pp. 7–28.

193 Cooper, A. M., Further developments in the clinical diagnosis of narcissistic personality disorder, in *Disorders of Narcissism: Diagnostic, Clinical and Empirical Implications*, edited by E. F. Ronningstram (Washington, DC, 1997), pp. 53–74.

194 Schlesinger, L., Pathological narcissism and serial homicide: review and case study. *Current Psychology* 17, 212–21 (1997).

195 Di Martino, A., Ross, K., Uddin, L. Q., Sklar, A. B., Castellanos, F. X. and Milham, M. P., Functional brain correlates of social and non-social processes in autism spectrum disorders: an activation likelihood estimation meta-analysis. *Biological Psychiatry* 65, 63–74 (2009).

196 Lombardo, M. V., Baron-Cohen, S., Belmonte, M. K. and Chakrabarti, B., Neural endophenotypes of social behaviour in autism spectrum conditions, in *Handbook of Social Neuroscience*, edited by J. Decety and J. Cacioppo (Oxford, in press).

197 Happé, F., Ehlers, S., Fletcher, P., Frith, U., Johansson, M., Gillberg, C., Dolan, R., Frackowiak, R. and Frith, C., 'Theory of mind' in the brain. Evidence from a PET scan study of Asperger syndrome. *Neuroreport* 8, 197–201 (1996).

198 Wang, A. T., Lee, S. S., Sigman, M. and Dapretto, M., Neural basis of irony comprehension in children with autism: the role of prosody and context. *Brain* 129, 932–43 (2006).

199 Wang, A. T., Lee, S. S., Sigman, M. and Dapretto, M., Reading affect in the face and voice: neural correlates of interpreting communicative intent in children and adolescents with autism spectrum disorders. *Archives of General Psychiatry* 64, 698–708 (2007).

200 Baron-Cohen, S. and Hammer, J., Parents of children with Asperger Syndrome: what is the cognitive phenotype? *Journal of Cognitive Neuroscience* 9, 548–54 (1997).

201 Baron-Cohen, S., Wheelwright, S., Hill, J., Raste, Y. and Plumb, I., The 'Reading the Mind in the Eyes' test revised version: A study with normal adults, and adults with Asperger Syndrome or High-Functioning Autism. *Journal of Child Psychology and Psychiatry* 42, 241–52 (2001).

202 Pelphrey, K. A., Morris, J. P. and McCarthy, G., Neural basis of eye gaze processing deficits in autism. *Brain* 128, 1038–48 (2005).

203 Herrington, J. D., Baron-Cohen, S., Wheelwright, S., Brammer, M., Singh, K. D., Bullmore, E. T. and Williams, S. C. R., The role of MT+/V5 during biological motion perception in Asperger Syndrome: an fMRI study. *Research in Autism Spectrum Disorders* 1, 14–27 (2007).

204 Pierce, K., Muller, R.-A., Ambrose, J., Allen, G. and Courchesne, E., Face processing occurs outside the 'fusiform face area' in autism: evidence from functional MRI. *Brain* 124, 2059–73 (2001).

205 Wang, A. T., Dapretto, M., Hariri, A. R., Sigman, M. and Bookheimer, S. Y., Neural correlates of facial affect processing in children and adolescents with autism spectrum disorder. *Journal of the American Academy of Child and Adolescent Psychiatry* 43, 481–90 (2004).

206 Ashwin, C., Baron-Cohen, S., O'Riordan, M., Wheelwright, S. and Bullmore, E. T., Differential activiation of the amygdala and the 'social brain' during fearful face-processing in Asperger Syndrome. *Neuropsychologia* 45, 2–14 (2007).

207 Corbett, B. A., Constantine, L. J., Hendren, R., Rocke, D. and Ozonoff, S., Examining executive functioning in children with autism spectrum disorder, attention deficit hyperactivity disorder and typical development. *Psychiatry Research* 166, 210–22 (2009).

208 Critchley, H. D., Daly, E. M., Bullmore, E. T., Williams, S. C. R., Van Amelsvoort, T., Robertson, D. M., Rowe, A., Phillips, M., McAlonan, G., Howlin, P. and Murphy, D. G., The functional neuroanatomy of social behaviour: changes in cerebral blood flow when people with autistic disorder process facial expressions. *Brain* 123, 2203–12 (2000).

209 Dalton, K. M., Nacewicz, B. M., Johnstone, T., Schaefer, H. S., Gernsbacher, M. A., Goldsmith, H. H., Alexander, A. L. and Davidson, R. J., Gaze fixation and the neural circuitry of face processing in autism. *Nature Neuroscience* 10, 1–8 (2005).

210 Grezes, J., Wicker, B., Berthoz, S. and de Gelder, B., A failure to grasp

the affective meaning of actions in autism spectrum disorder subjects. *Neuropsychologia* 47, 1816–25 (2009).

211 Pelphrey, K. A., Morris, J. P., McCarthy, G. and Labar, K. S., Perception of dynamic changes in facial affect and identity in autism. *Social Cognitive and Affective Neuroscience* 2, 140–9 (2007).

212 Dinstein, I., Thomas, C., Humphreys, K., Minshew, N., Behrmann, M. and Heeger, D. J., Normal movement selectivity in autism. *Neuron* 66, 461–9 (2010).

213 Southgate, V. and Hamilton, A. F., Unbroken mirrors: challenging a theory of autism. *Trends in Cognitive Sciences* 12, 225–9 (2008).

214 Abell, F., Happé, F. R. and Frith, U., Do triangles play tricks? Attribution of mental states to animated shapes in normal and abnormal development. *Cognitive Development* 15, 1–16 (2000).

215 Castelli, F., Frith, C., Happé, F. R., and Frith, U., Autism, Asperger syndrome and brain mechanisms for the attribution of mental states to animated shapes. *Brain* 125, 1839–49 (2002).

216 Kana, R. K., Keller, T. A., Cherkassky, V. L., Minshew, N. J. and Just, M. A., Atypical frontal-posterior synchronization of Theory of Mind regions in autism during mental state attribution. *Social Neuroscience* 4, 135–52 (2009).

217 Hill, E., Berthoz, S. and Frith, U., Brief report: cognitive processing of own emotions in individuals with autistic spectrum disorder and in their relatives. *Journal of Autism and Developmental Disorders* 34, 229–35 (2004).

218 Lombardo, M. V. and Baron-Cohen, S., Unraveling the paradox of the autistic self. *Wiley Interdisciplinary Reviews: Cognitive Science* 1, 393–403 (2010).

219 Lombardo, M. V., Barnes, J. L., Wheelwright, S. and Baron-Cohen, S., Self-referential cognition and empathy in autism. *Public Library of Science One* 2, e883 (2007).

220 Williams, D. M. and Happé, F. R., What did I say? Versus what did I think? Attributing false beliefs to self amongst children with and without autism. *Journal of Autism and Developmental Disorders* 39, 865–73 (2009).

221 Silani, G., Bird, G., Brindley, R., Singer, T., Frith, C. and Frith, U., Levels of emotional awareness and autism: an fMRI study. *Social Neuroscience* 3, 97–112 (2008).

222 Ernst, M., Zametkin, A. J., Matochik, J. A., Pascualvaca, D. and Cohen, R. M., Low medial prefrontal dopaminergic activity in autistic children. *Lancet* 350, 638 (1997).

223 Murphy, D. G., Daly, E., Schmitz, N., Toal, F., Murphy, K., Curran, S., Erlandsson, K., Eersels, J., Kerwin, R., Ell, P. and Travis, M., Cortical serotonin 5-HT2A receptor binding and social communication in adults with Asperger's syndrome: an in vivo SPECT study. *American Journal of Psychiatry* 163, 934–6 (2006).

224 Haznedar, M. M., Buchsbaum, M. S., Wei, T. C., Hof, P. R., Cartwright, C., Bienstock, C. A. and Hollander, E., Limbic circuitry in patients with autism spectrum disorders studied with positron emission tomography and magnetic resonance imaging. *American Journal of Psychiatry* 157, 1994–2001 (2000).

225 Ohnishi, T., Matsuda, H., Hashimoto, T., Kunihiro, T., Nishikawa, M., Uema, T. and Sasaki, M., Abnormal regional cerebral blood flow in childhood autism. *Brain* 123, 1838–44 (2000).

226 Kennedy, D. P. and Courchesne, E., The intrinsic functional organization of the brain is altered in autism. *Neuroimage* 39, 1877–85 (2008).

227 Kennedy, D. P., Redcay, E. and Courchesne, E., Failing to deactivate: resting functional abnormalities in autism. *Proceedings of the National Academy of Sciences of the United States of America* 103, 8275–80 (2006).

228 Lombardo, M. V., Chakrabarti, B., Bullmore, E. T., Sadek, S. A., Pasco, G., Wheelwright, S. J., Suckling, J. and Baron-Cohen, S., Atypical neural self-representation in autism. *Brain* 133, 611–24 (2010).

229 Minio-Paluello, I., Baron-Cohen, S., Avenanti, A., Walsh, V. and Aglioti, S. M., Absence of embodied empathy during pain observation in Asperger syndrome. *Biological Psychiatry* 65, 55–62 (2009).

230 Tomlin, D., Kayali, M. A., King-Casas, B., Anen, C., Camerer, C. F., Quartz, S. R. and Montague, P. R., Agent-specific responses in the cingulate cortex during economic exchanges. *Science* 312, 1047–50 (2006).

231 Frith, C. D. and Frith, U., The self and its reputation in autism. *Neuron* 57, 331–2 (2008).

232 Chiu, P. H., Kayali, M. A., Kishida, K. T., Tomlin, D., Klinger, L. G., Klinger, M. R. and Montague, P. R., Self responses along cingulate cortex reveal quantitative neural phenotype for high-functioning autism. *Neuron* 57, 463–73 (2008).

233 Lombardo, M. V., Chakrabarti, B., Bullmore, E. T., Wheelwright, S., Sadek, S., Suckling, J. MRC Aims Consortium and Baron-Cohen, S., Atypical neural self representation in autism. *Brain* 133, 611–24 (2010).

234 Baron-Cohen, S., Ashwin, E., Ashwin, C., Tavassoli, T. and Chakrabarti,

B., Talent in autism: hyper-systemizing, hyper-attention to detail and sensory hypersensitivity. *Philosophical Transactions of the Royal Society of London B. Biological Sciences* 364, 1377–83 (2009).

235 Baron-Cohen, S., The hyper-systemizing, assortative mating theory of autism. *Progress in Neuropsychopharmacology and Biological Psychiatry* 30, 865–72 (2006).

236 Tammet, D., *Born on a Blue Day* (London, 2006).

237 Baron-Cohen, S., Bor, D., Billington, J., Asher, J., Wheelwright, S. and Ashwin, C., Savant memory in a man with colour-number synaesthesia and Asperger Syndrome. *Journal of Consciousness Studies* 14, 237–51 (2007).

238 Available at http://www.lisaperini.it/.

239 Ockelford, A., *In the Key of Genius: The Extraordinary Life of Derek Paravicini* (London, 2007).

240 Myers, P., Baron-Cohen, S. and Wheelwright, S., *An Exact Mind* (London, 2004).

241 Baron-Cohen, S., Richler, J., Bisarya, D., Gurunathan, N. and Wheelwright, S., The Systemising Quotient (SQ): An investigation of adults with Asperger Syndrome or High Functioning Autism and normal sex differences. *Philosophical Transactions of the Royal Society* 358, 361–74 (2003).

242 Wheelwright, S., Baron-Cohen, S., Goldenfeld, N., Delaney, J., Fine, D., Smith, R., Weil, L. and Wakabayashi, A., Predicting Autism Spectrum Quotient (AQ) from the Systemizing Quotient-Revised (SQ-R) and Empathy Quotient (EQ). *Brain Research* 1079, 47–56 (2006).

243 Lawson, J., Baron-Cohen, S. and Wheelwright, S., Empathising and systemising in adults with and without Asperger Syndrome. *Journal of Autism and Developmental Disorders* 34, 301–10 (2004).

244 Baron-Cohen, S., *Autism and Asperger Syndrome* (Oxford, 2008).

245 Fitzgerald, M. and O'Brien, B., *Genius Genes: How Asperger Talents Changed the World* (Shawnee Mission, Kans., 2007).

246 Kanner, L., Autistic disturbance of affective contact. *Nervous Child* 2, 217–50 (1943).

247 Blastland, M., *Joe: The Only Boy in the World* (London, 2006).

248 Losh, M. and Piven, J., Social cognition and the broad autism phenotype: identifying genetically meaningful phenotypes. *Journal of Child Psychology and Psychiatry* 48, 105–12 (2007).

249 Baron-Cohen, S., Ring, H., Chitnis, X., Wheelwright, S., Gregory, L., Williams, S., Brammer, M. and Bullmore, E., fMRI of parents of

children with Asperger Syndrome: a pilot study. *Brain Cognition* **61**, 122–30 (2006).

250 Wootton, J. M., Frick, P. J., Shelton, K. K. and Silverthorn, P., Ineffective parenting and childhood conduct problems: the moderating role of callous-unemotional traits. *Journal of Consulting and Clinical Psychology* **65**, 301–08 (1997).

251 Cicchetti, D., Cummings, E. M., Greenberg, M. T. and Marvin, R. S., An organizational perspective on attachment beyond infancy, in *Attachment in the Preschool Years*, edited by Greenberg, M., Cicchetti, D. and Cummings, M. (Chicago, 1990), pp. 3–50.

252 Davis, M. H., Luce, C. and Kraus, S. J., The heritability of characteristics associated with dispositional empathy. *Journal of Personality and Social Psychology* **62**, 369–91 (1994).

253 Loehlin, J. C. and Nichols, R. C., *Heredity, Environment, and Personality* (Austin, Tex., 1976).

254 Matthews, K. A., Batson, C. D., Horn, J. and Rosenman, R. H., 'Principles in his nature which interest him in the fortune of others . . .': The heritability of empathic concern for others. *Journal of Personality and Social Psychology* **49**, 237–47 (1981).

255 Hughes, C., Jaffee, S. R., Happé, F. R.,, Taylor, A., Caspi, A. and Moffitt, T. E., Origins of individual differences in theory of mind: from nature to nurture? *Child Development* **76**, 356–70 (2005).

256 Ronald, A., Happé, F. R.,, Price, T. S., Baron-Cohen, S. and Plomin, R., Phenotypic and genetic overlap between autistic traits at the extremes of the general population. *Journal of the American Academy of Child and Adolescent Psychiatry* **45**, 1206–14 (2006).

257 Zahn-Waxler, C., Radke-Yarrow, M., Wagner, E. and Chapman, M., Development of concern for others. *Developmental Psychology* **28**, 126–36 (1992).

258 Knafo, A., Zahn-Waxler, C., Van Hulle, C., Robinson, J. L. and Rhee, S. H., The developmental origins of a disposition toward empathy: Genetic and environmental contributions. *Emotion* **8**, 737–52 (2008).

259 Szatmari, P., Georgiades, S., Duku, E., Zwaigenbaum, L., Goldberg, J. and Bennett, T., Alexithymia in parents of children with autism spectrum disorder. *Journal of Autism and Developmental Disorders* **38**, 1859–65 (2008).

260 Blonigen, D. M., Carlson, S. R., Krueger, R. F. and Patrick, C. J., A twin study of self-reported psychopathic personality traits. *Personality and Individual Differences* **35**, 179–97 (2003).

261 Viding, E., Blair, R. J., Moffitt, T. E. and Plomin, R., Evidence for substantial genetic risk for psychopathy in 7-year-olds. *Journal of Child Psychology and Psychiatry* **46**, 592–7 (2005).

262 Rhee, S. H. and Waldman, I. D., Genetic and environmental influences on antisocial behavior: a meta-analysis of twin and adoption studies. *Psychological Bulletin* **128** (3), 490–529 (2002).

263 Zanarini, M. C., Williams, A. A., Lewis, R. E., Reich, R. B., Vera, S. C., Marino, M. F., Levin, A., Yong, L. and Frankenburg, F. R., Reported pathological childhood experiences associated with the development of borderline personality disorder. *American Journal of Psychiatry* **154**, 1101–06 (1997).

264 Links, P. S., Steiner, M., Offord, D. R. and Eppel, A., Characteristics of borderline personality disorder: a Canadian study. *Canadian Journal of Psychiatry* **33**, 336–40 (1988).

265 Soloff, P. H. and Millward, J. W., Developmental histories of borderline patients. *Comprehensive Psychiatry* **24**, 574–88 (1983).

266 Zanarini, M. C., Gunderson, J. G., Marino, M. F., Schwartz, E. O. and Frankenburg, F. R., Childhood experiences of borderline patients. *Comprehensive Psychiatry* **30**, 18–25 (1989).

267 Gunderson, J. G. and Englund, D. W., Characterizing the families of borderlines. A review of the literature. *Psychiatric Clinics of North America* **4**, 159–68 (1981).

268 Zweig-Frank, H. and Paris, J., Parents' emotional neglect and overprotection according to the recollections of patients with borderline personality disorder. *American Journal of Psychiatry* **148**, 648–51 (1991).

269 Trull, T. J., Sher, K. J., Minks-Brown, C., Durbin, J. and Burr, R., Borderline personality disorder and substance use disorders: a review and integration. *Clinical Psychology Review* **20**, 235–53 (2000).

270 Loranger, A. W., Oldham, J. M. and Tulis, E. H., Familial transmission of DSM-III borderline personality disorder. *Archives of General Psychiatry* **39**, 795–9 (1982).

271 Torgersen, S., Genetics of patients with borderline personality disorder. *Psychiatric Clinics of North America* **23**, 1–9 (2000).

272 Adolphs, R., Spezio, M. L., Parlier, M. and Piven, J., Distinct face-processing strategies in parents of autistic children. *Current Biology* **18**, 1090–3 (2008).

273 Dorris, L., Espie, C. A. E., Knott, F. and Salt, J., Mindreading difficulties in the siblings of people with Asperger's Syndrome: evidence for a genetic influence in the abnormal development of a specific cognitive

domain. *Journal of Child Psychology and Psychiatry* 45, 412–18 (2004).

274 Losh, M., Adolphs, R., Poe, M. D., Couture, S., Penn, D., Baranek, G. T. and Piven, J., Neuropsychological profile of autism and the broad autism phenotype. *Archives of General Psychiatry* 66 (5), 518–26 (2009).

275 Hoekstra, R., Bartels, M., Hudziak, J., Van Beijsterveldt, T. and Boomsma, D., Genetic and environmental covariation between autistic traits and behavioral problems. *Twin Research and Human Genetics* 10 (6), 853–60 (2007).

276 Bailey, A., Le Couteur, A., Gottesman, I., Bolton, P., Simmonoff, E., Yuzda, E. and Rutter, M., Autism as a strongly genetic disorder: evidence from a British twin study. *Psychological Medicine* 25, 63–77 (1995).

277 Folstein, S. and Rutter, M., Infantile autism: A genetic study of 21 twin pairs. *Journal of Child Psycholology and Psychiatry* 18, 297–321 (1977).

278 Bell, C., Abrams, J. and Nutt, D., Tryptophan depletion and its implications for psychiatry. *British Journal of Psychiatry* 178, 399–405 (2001).

279 Caspi, A. and Silva, P. A., Temperamental qualities at age three predict personality traits in young adulthood: longitudinal evidence from a birth cohort. *Child Development* 66, 486–98 (1995).

280 Caspi, A., McClay, J., Moffitt, T. E., Mill, J., Martin, J., Craig, I. W., Taylor, A. and Poulton, R., Role of genotype in the cycle of violence in maltreated children. *Science* 297, 851–4 (2002).

281 Buckholtz, J. W. and Meyer-Lindenberg, A., MAOA and the neurogenetic architecture of human aggression. *Trends in Neurosciences* 31, 120–9 (2008).

282 Meyer-Lindenberg, A., Buckholtz, J. W., Kolachana, B., Hariri, A. R., Pezawas, L., Blasi, G., Wabnitz, A., Honea, R., Verchinski, B., Callicott, J. H., Egan, M., Mattay, V. and Weinberger, D. R., Neural mechanisms of genetic risk for impulsivity and violence in humans. *Proceedings of the National Academy of Sciences of the United States of America* 103, 6269–74 (2006).

283 Hariri, A. R., Drabant, E. M., Munoz, K. E., Kolachana, B. S., Mattay, V. S., Egan, M. F. and Weinberger, D. R., A susceptibility gene for affective disorders and the response of the human amygdala. *Archives of General Psychiatry* 62, 146–52 (2005).

284 Hariri, A. R., Mattay, V. S., Tessitore, A., Kolachana, B., Fera, F., Goldman, D., Egan, M. and Weinberger, D. R., Serotonin transporter

genetic variation and the response of the human amygdala. *Science* 297, 400–3 (2002).

285 Takahashi, H., Takano, H., Kodaka, F., Arakawa, R., Yamada, M., Otsuka, T., Hirano, Y., Kikyo, H., Okubo, Y., Kato, M., Obata, T., Ito, H. and Suhara, T., Contribution of dopamine D1 and D2 receptors to amygdala activity in humans. *Journal of Neuroscience* 30, 3043–7 (2010).

286 Takahashi, H., Yahata, N., Koeda, M., Takano, A., Asai, K., Suhara, T. and Okubo, Y., Effects of dopaminergic and serotonergic manipulation on emotional processing: a pharmacological fMRI study. *Neuroimage* 27 (4), 991–1001 (2005).

287 Kempton, M. J., Haldane, M., Jogia, J., Christodoulou, T., Powell, J., Collier, D., Williams, S. C. and Frangou, S., The effects of gender and COMT Val158Met polymorphism on fearful facial affect recognition: a fMRI study. *International Journal of Neuropsychopharmacology* 12, 371–81 (2009).

288 Meyer-Lindenberg, A., Kolachana, B., Gold, B., Olsh, A., Nicodemus, K. K., Mattay, V., Dean, M. and Weinberger, D. R., Genetic variants in AVPR1A linked to autism predict amygdala activation and personality traits in healthy humans. *Molecular Psychiatry* 14 (10), 968–75 (2009).

289 Kawagoe, R., Takikawa, Y. and Hikosaka, O., Expectation of reward modulates cognitive signals in the basal ganglia. *Nature Neuroscience* 1, 411–16 (1998).

290 Schultz, R., Gauthier, I., Klin, A., Fulbright, R. K., Anderson, A., Volkmar, F., Skudlarski, P., Lacadie, C., Cohen, D. and Gore, J. C., Abnormal ventral temporal cortical activity among individuals with autism and Asperger Syndrome during face discrimination among individuals with autism and Asperger Syndrome. *Archives of General Psychiatry* 57, 331–40 (2000).

291 Chakrabarti, B., Kent, L., Suckling, J., Bullmore, E. T. and Baron-Cohen, S., Variations in the human cannabinoid receptor (CNR1) gene modulate striatal response to happy faces. *European Journal of Neuroscience* 23, 1944–8 (2006).

292 Domschke, K., Dannlowski, U., Ohrmann, P., Lawford, B., Bauer, J., Kugel, H., Heindel, W., Young, R., Morris, P., Arolt, V., Deckert, J., Suslow, T. and Baune, B. T., Cannabinoid receptor 1 (CNR1) gene: impact on antidepressant treatment response and emotion processing in major depression. *European Neuropsychopharmacology* 18, 751–9 (2008).

293 Wakabayashi, A., Baron-Cohen, S. and Wheelwright, S., Individual and gender differences in Empathizing and Systemizing: measurement of individual differences by the Empathy Quotient (EQ) and the Systemizing Quotient (SQ). *Shinrigaku Kenkyu* 77, 271–7 (2006).

294 Baron-Cohen, S., Lutchmaya, S. and Knickmeyer, R., *Prenatal Testosterone In Mind: Amniotic Fluid Studies* (Cambridge, Mass., 2004).

295 Chapman, E., Baron-Cohen, S., Auyeung, B., Knickmeyer, R., Taylor, K. and Hackett, G., Foetal testosterone and empathy: evidence from the Empathy Quotient (EQ) and the 'Reading the Mind in the Eyes' test. *Social Neuroscience* 1, 135–48 (2006).

296 Young, L. J. and Wang, Z., The neurobiology of pair bonding. *Nature Neuroscience* 7, 1048–54 (2004).

297 Donaldson, Z. R. and Young, L. J., Oxytocin, vasopressin, and the neurogenetics of sociality. *Science* 322, 900–04 (2008).

298 Winslow, J. T. and Insel, T. R., Neuroendocrine basis of social recognition. *Current Opinions in Neurobiology* 14, 248–53 (2004).

299 Domes, G., Heinrichs, M., Michel, A., Berger, C. and Herpertz, S. C., Oxytocin improves 'mind-reading' in humans. *Biological Psychiatry* 61, 731–3 (2007).

300 Ebstein, R. P., Israel, S., Lerer, E., Uzefovsky, F., Shalev, I., Gritsenko, I., Riebold, M., Salomon, S. and Yirmiya, N., Arginine vasopressin and oxytocin modulate human social behavior. *Annals of the New York Academy of Sciences* 1167, 87–102 (2009).

301 Zak, P. J., Stanton, A. A. and Ahmadi, S., Oxytocin increases generosity in humans. *Public Library of Science One* 2, e1128 (2007).

302 Kosfeld, M., Heinrichs, M., Zak, P. J., Fischbacher, U. and Fehr, E., Oxytocin increases trust in humans. *Nature* 435, 673–6 (2005).

303 Levine, A., Zagoory-Sharon, O., Feldman, R. and Weller, A., Oxytocin during pregnancy and early postpartum: individual patterns and maternal–fetal attachment. *Peptides* 28, 1162–9 (2007).

304 Chakrabarti, B., Dudbridge, F., Kent, L., Wheelwright, S., Hill-Cawthorne, G., Allison, C., Banerjee-Basu, S. and Baron-Cohen, S., Genes related to sex steroids, neural growth, and social-emotional behavior are associated with autistic traits, empathy, and Asperger syndrome. *Autism Research* 2, 157–77 (2009).

305 Jeon, D., Kim, S., Chetana, M., Jo, D., Ruley, H. E., Lin, S. Y., Rabah, D., Kinet, J. P. and Shin, H. S., Observational fear learning involves affective pain system and Cav1.2 Ca2+ channels in ACC. *Nature Neuroscience* 13, 482–8 (2010).

306 Mednick, S. A. and Kandel, E. S., Congenital determinants of violence.

Bulletin of the American Academy of Psychiatry Law **16**, 101–9 (1988).

307 Raine, A., Annotation: the role of prefrontal deficits, low autonomic arousal, and early health factors in the development of antisocial and aggressive behavior in children. *Journal of Child Psychology and Psychiatry* **43**, 417–34 (2002).

308 de Waal, F., *The Age of Empathy: Nature's Lessons For a Kinder Society* (New York, 2009).

309 de Waal, F., Leimgruber, K. and Greenberg, A. R., Giving is self-rewarding for monkeys. *Proceedings of the National Academy of Sciences of the United States of America* **105** 13685–9 (2008).

310 Mineka, S., Davidson, M., Cook, M. and Keir, R., Observational conditioning of snake fear in rhesus monkeys. *Journal of Abnormal Psychology* **93**, 355–72 (1984).

311 Harlow, H. F., Dodsworth, R. O. and Harlow, M. K., Total social isolation in monkeys. *Proceedings of the National Academy of Sciences of the United States of America* **54**, 90–7 (1965).

312 Rice, G. E. and Gainer, P., 'Altruism' in the albino rat. *Journal of Comparative and Physiological Psychology* **55**, 123–5 (1962).

313 Masserman, J. H., Wechkin, S. and Terris, W., 'Altruistic' behavior in rhesus monkeys. *American Journal of Psychiatry* **121**, 584–5 (1964).

314 Povinelli, D. J., Can animals empathize? *Scientific American Presents: Exploring Intelligence* **9**, 67, 72–5 (1998).

315 Golan, O., Baron-Cohen, S., Wheelwright, S. and Hill, J. J., Systemising empathy: teaching adults with Asperger Syndrome to recognise complex emotions using interactive multi-media. *Development and Psychopathology* **18**, 589–615 (2006).

316 Golan, O., Baron-Cohen, S., Ashwin, E., Granader, Y., McClintock, S., Day, K. and Leggett, V., Enhancing emotion recognition in children with autism spectrum conditions: an intervention using animated vehicles with real emotional faces. *Journal of Autism and Developmental Disorders* **40**, 269–79 (2010).

317 Hollander, E., Bartz, J., Chaplin, W., Phillips, A., Sumner, J., Soorya, L., Anagnostou, E. and Wasserman, S., Oxytocin increases retention of social cognition in autism. *Biological Psychiatry* **61**, 498–503 (2007).

318 Baron-Cohen, S. and Machlis, A., Intense negotiations will not necessarily work: intense empathy will. *The Jewish Chronicle*, 5 June 2009, p.31.

319 Treasure, J. L., Getting beneath the phenotype of anorexia nervosa: the search for viable endophenotypes and genotypes. *Canadian Journal of Psychiatry* **52**, 212–19 (2007).

320 Gillberg, C., The Emanuel Miller Lecture, 1991: Autism and autistic-like conditions: subclasses among disorders of empathy. *Journal of Child Psychology and Psychiatry* 33, 813–42 (1992).

321 *Daily Mail*, online edition, 22 September 2009.

322 Arendt, H., *Eichmann in Jerusalem: A Report on the Banality of Evil* (New York, 1963).

323 Haslam, S. A. and Reicher, S. D., Questioning the banality of evil. *The Psychologist* 21, 16–19 (2008).

324 Milgram, S., *Obedience to Authority: An Experimental View* (New York, 1974).

325 Zimbardo, P., *The Lucifer Effect: Understanding How Good People Turn Evil* (New York, 2007).

326 Browning, C. R., *Ordinary Men: Reserve Police Battalion 101 and the Final Solution in Poland* (London, 2001).

327 Cesarini, D., *Eichmann: His Life and Crimes* (London, 2004).

328 Evans, R., *In Hitler's Shadow* (London, 1989).

329 *Guardian*, 12 May 2004.

330 *Guardian*, 18 July 2003.

331 Auyeung, B., Baron-Cohen, S., Chapman, E., Knickmeyer, R., Taylor, K. and Hackett, G., Foetal testosterone and the Child Systemizing Quotient (SQ-C). *European Journal of Endrocrinology* 155, 123–30 (2006).

332 *Daily Telegraph*, 19 March 2009.

333 *Slate*, 20 April 2004.

334 CNN News, 28 July 2009.

335 *The Globe and Mail*, Ontario edition, 29 July 2009.

336 Burnett, S. and Blakemore, S. J., The development of adolescent social cognition. *Annals of the New York Academy of Sciences* 1167, 51–6 (2009).

337 Ashwin, C., Chapman, E., Colle, L. and Baron-Cohen, S., Impaired recognition of negative basic emotions in autism: a test of the amygdala theory. *Social Neuroscience* 1, 349–63 (2006).

338 Owens, G., Granader, Y., Humphrey, A. and Baron-Cohen, S., LEGO® therapy and the social use of language programme: an evaluation of two social skills interventions for children with high functioning autism and Asperger Syndrome. *Journal of Autism and Developmental Disorders* 38, 1944–57 (2008).

339 BBC Television, 6 December 2009.

340 *Time Magazine*, 26 September 1977.

341 Harari, H., Shamay-Tsoory, S., Ravid, M., Levkovitz, Y. 'Double dissociation between cognitive and affective empathy in borderline personality disorder'. *Psychiatry Research*, 175, 277–279 (2010).

342 Dziobek, I., Rogers, K., Fleck, S., Bahnemann, M., Heekeren, H., Wolf, O., and Convit, A., 'Dissociation of Cognitive and Emotional Empathy in Adults with Asperger Syndrome Using the Multifaceted Empathy Test (MET)'. *Journal of Autism and Developmental Disorders*, 38, 464–473 (2008).

343 Schwenck, C., et al 'Empathy in children with autism and conduct disorder: group-specific profiles and developmental aspects'. *Journal of Child Psychology and Psychiatry*, 26 November (2011).

Index

Page references in *italic* indicate figures.

abandonment 44, 52, 129, 144
  fears 35, 41, 42, 43, 144
aborization 60
acetylcholine 151
adrenocorticotropic hormone
  (ACTH) 59
affective empathy (response stage)
  12, 85, 90–91, *108*, 149
aggression 45, 49, 54, 55
  genes for 92–3
  reactive 55, 59–60, 155
  see also violence
AI (anterior insula) 21, 24–5,
  59, 71
alexithymia 72
Allison, Carrie 15
aloneness
  borderlines' intolerance of 35, 41
  desire to be alone 18
  see also abandonment
altruism 100, 128, 149
amniocentesis 93
amorality 54
amygdala 21, 28, 44, 45, 56, 57,
  59, 60, 71, 96, 150
anger 32–3
  recognition of 24
  see also rage
animal research
  empathy in animals 99–100

MAOA (monoamine oxidase-A)
  gene 93
Animations Test 71–2
anoxia 99
anterior cingulate cortex 93
  caudal (cACC) 21, 24, 25
anterior insula (AI) 21, 24–5,
  59, 71
anterior temporal lobe (ATL) 150
anti-Semitism 119, 131
Antisocial Personality Disorder *see*
  Psychopathic/Antisocial
  Personality Disorder
anxiety
  abandonment 35, 41, 42, 43,
  144
  BIS model 55
  a psychopath's lack of 48, 55
AQ (Autism Spectrum Quotient)
  97–6
Archimedes 78
Arendt, Hannah 114, 116
arginine vasopressin (AVP) 93–4
arginine vasopressin receptor 1A
  gene (AVPR 1A) 93
Armenians 9–10
ARNT1 gene 98
ARNT2 gene 98
art, of people with Asperger
  Syndrome 75, 76